JUL 2008   35.00

P9-DED-641

THE THIRTEEN COLONIES

New York

CRAIG A. DOHERTY

KATHERINE M. DOHERTY

HIGHLAND PARK PUBLIC LIBRARY
494 LAUREL AVE.
HIGHLAND PARK, IL 60035-2690
847-432-0216

Facts On File, Inc.

J
974.7
D655

New York

Copyright © 2005 by Craig A. Doherty and Katherine M. Doherty

Maps and graphs copyright © 2005 by Facts On File, Inc.
Captions copyright © 2005 by Facts On File, Inc.

All rights reserved. No part of this book may be reproduced or utilized in any form or by any means, electronic or mechanical, including photocopying, recording, or by any information storage or retrieval systems, without permission in writing from the publisher. For information contact:

Facts On File, Inc.
132 West 31st Street
New York NY 10001

Library of Congress Cataloging-in-Publication Data
Doherty, Craig A.
 New York / Craig A. Doherty and Katherine M. Doherty.
  p. cm. — (Thirteen colonies)
 Includes bibliographical references (p.) and index.
 ISBN 0-8160-5410-X (acid-free paper)
  1. New York (State)—History—Colonial period, ca. 1600–1775—Juvenile literature. 2. New York (State)—History—1775–1865—Juvenile literature. I. Doherty, Katherine M. II. Title.

   F122.D675 2004
   974.7'02—dc22   2004003791

Facts On File books are available at special discounts when purchased in bulk quantities for businesses, associations, institutions, or sales promotions. Please call our Special Sales Department in New York at (212) 967-8800 or (800) 322-8755.

You can find Facts On File on the World Wide Web at http://www.factsonfile.com

Text design by Erika K. Arroyo
Cover design by Semadar Megged
Maps and graphs by Sholto Ainslie

Printed in the United States of America

VB FOF 10 9 8 7 6 5 4 3 2 1

This book is printed on acid-free paper.

Contents

Note on Photos

Many of the illustrations and photographs used in this book are old, historical images. The quality of the prints is not always up to current standards, as in some cases the originals are from old or poor-quality negatives or are damaged. The content of the illustrations, however, made their inclusion important despite problems in reproduction.

Introduction

In the 11th century, Vikings from Scandinavia sailed to North America. They explored the Atlantic coast and set up a few small settlements. In Newfoundland and Nova Scotia, Canada, archaeologists have found traces of these settlements. No one knows for sure why they did not establish permanent colonies. It may have been that it was too far away from their homeland. At about the same time, many Scandinavians were involved with raiding and establishing settlements along the coasts of what are now Great Britain and France. This may have offered greater rewards than traveling all the way to North America.

When the western part of the Roman Empire fell in 476, Europe lapsed into a period of almost 1,000 years of wars, plagues, and hardship. This period of European history is often referred to as the Dark Ages or Middle Ages. Communication between the different parts of Europe was almost nonexistent. If other Europeans knew about the Vikings' explorations westward, they left no record of it. Between the time of Viking exploration and Christopher Columbus's 1492 journey, Europe underwent many changes.

By the 15th century, Europe had experienced many advances. Trade within the area and with the Far East had created prosperity for the governments and many wealthy people. The Catholic Church had become a rich and powerful institution. Although wars would be fought and governments would come and go, the countries of Western Europe had become fairly strong. During this time, Europe rediscovered many of the arts and sciences that had

Vikings explored the Atlantic coast of North America in ships similar to this one. *(National Archives of Canada)*

existed before the fall of Rome. They also learned much from their trade with the Near and Far East. Historians refer to this time as the Renaissance, which means "rebirth."

At this time, some members of the Catholic Church did not like the direction the church was going. People such as Martin Luther and John Calvin spoke out against the church. They soon gained a number of followers who decided that they would protest and form their own churches. The members of these new churches were called Protestants. The movement to establish these new churches is called the Protestant Reformation. It would have a big impact on America as many Protestant groups would leave Europe so they could worship the way they wanted to.

In addition to religious dissent, problems arose with the overland trade routes to the Far East. The Ottoman Turks took control of the lands in the Middle East and disrupted trade. It was at this time that European explorers began trying to find a water route to the Far East. The explorers first sailed around Africa. Then an Italian named Christopher Columbus convinced the king and queen of Spain that it would be shorter to sail west to Asia rather than go around Africa. Most sailors and educated people at the time knew the world was round. However, Columbus made two errors in his calculations. First, he did not realize just how big the Earth is, and second, he did not know that the continents of North and South America blocked a westward route to Asia.

When Columbus made landfall in 1492, he believed that he was in the Indies, as the Far East was called at the time. For a period of time after Columbus, the Spanish controlled the seas and the exploration of what was called the New World. England tried to compete with the Spanish on the high seas, but their ships were no match for the floating fortresses of the Spanish Armada. These heavy ships, known as galleons, ruled the Atlantic.

In 1588, that all changed. A fleet of English ships fought a series of battles in which their smaller but faster and more maneuverable ships finally defeated the Spanish Armada. This opened up the New World to anyone willing to cross the ocean. Portugal, Holland, France, and England all funded voyages of exploration to the New World. In North America, the French explored the far north. The Spanish had already established colonies in what are now Florida, most of the Caribbean, and much of

Depicted in this painting, Christopher Columbus completed three additional voyages to the Americas after his initial trip in search of a westward route to Asia in 1492. *(Library of Congress, Prints and Photographs Division [LC-USZ62-103980])*

Central and South America. The Dutch bought Manhattan and would establish what would become New York, as well as various islands in the Caribbean and lands in South America. The English claimed most of the east coast of North America and set about creating colonies in a variety of ways.

Companies were formed in England and given royal charters to set up colonies. Some of the companies sent out military and trade expeditions to find gold and other riches. They employed men such as John Smith, Bartholomew Gosnold, and others to explore the lands they had been granted. Other companies found groups of Protestants who wanted to leave England and worked out deals that let them establish colonies. No matter what circumstances a colony was established under, the first settlers suffered hardships as

Composed of large, heavy ships known as galleons, the Spanish Armada, seen here in an early 17th-century engraving, was a formidable enemy of the English during the 16th century. The Spanish ruled the seas with this floating fortress until their defeat by the more maneuverable English fleet. *(Library of Congress, Prints and Photographs Division [LC-USZ62-86540])*

they tried to build communities in what to them was a wilderness. They also had to deal with the people who were already there.

Native Americans lived in every corner of the Americas. There were vast and complex civilizations in Central and South America. The city that is now known as Cahokia was located along the Mississippi River in what is today Illinois and may have had as many as 50,000 residents. The people of Cahokia built huge earthen mounds that can still be seen today. There has been a lot of speculation as to the total population of Native Americans in 1492. Some have put the number as high as 40 million people.

Most of the early explorers encountered Native Americans. They often wrote descriptions of them for the people of Europe. They also kidnapped a few of these people, took them back to Europe, and put them on display. Despite the number of Native Americans, the Europeans still claimed the land as their own. The rulers of Europe and the Catholic Church at the time felt they had a right to take any lands they wanted from people who did not share their level of technology and who were not Christians.

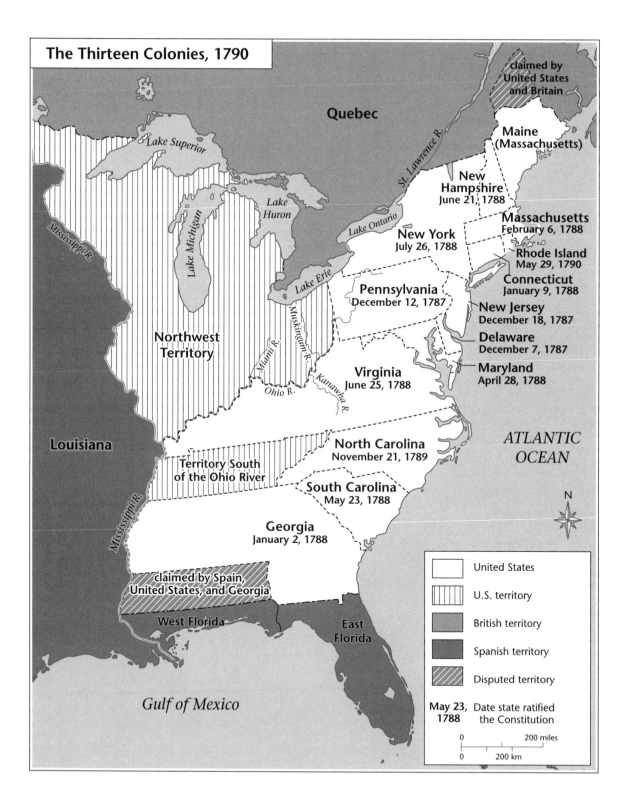

The Thirteen Colonies, 1790

Quebec

Lake Superior

Lake Michigan

Lake Huron

Lake Ontario

Lake Erie

Mississippi R.

Northwest
Territory

Louisiana

Miami R.

Muskingum R.

Ohio R.

Kanawha R.

St. Lawrence R.

claimed by
United States
and Britain

Maine
(Massachusetts)

New
Hampshire
June 21, 1788

New York
July 26, 1788

Massachusetts
February 6, 1788

Rhode Island
May 29, 1790

Connecticut
January 9, 1788

Pennsylvania
December 12, 1787

New Jersey
December 18, 1787

Delaware
December 7, 1787

Maryland
April 28, 1788

Virginia
June 25, 1788

ATLANTIC
OCEAN

Territory South
of the Ohio River

North Carolina
November 21, 1789

South Carolina
May 23, 1788

Georgia
January 2, 1788

claimed by Spain,
United States, and Georgia

West Florida

East
Florida

Mississippi R.

N

Gulf of Mexico

	United States
	U.S. territory
	British territory
	Spanish territory
	Disputed territory

May 23,
1788   Date state ratified
the Constitution

0   200 miles

0   200 km

First Contacts

EARLY EXPLORERS

After Christopher Columbus's voyage in 1492, there was a brief period of interest by other European countries in his discoveries. In 1497 and 1498, John Cabot, an Italian, sailed to North America for England. He was probably the first European since the Vikings to see the Northeast coast of North America. He claimed all the land from Chesapeake Bay north to Newfoundland and Labrador for the king of England, Henry VII. The English waited more than 100 years before they did anything about the lands claimed by Cabot. The Dutch were the first Europeans to settle what is now New York.

During the 16th century, small numbers of European fishermen began sailing to the rich fishing grounds off the coast of North America. Some of these people probably landed along the coast and set up temporary camps. However, there are very few records of this. The next recorded exploration of the area that became New York was by Giovanni da Verrazano, an Italian navigator who sailed along the North American coast for France in 1525. Verrazano wrote of anchoring in the narrow channel between what is now known as Lower and Upper New York Bay. This channel is now called the Verrazano Narrows. Some of Verrazano's men are reported to have gone ashore in the area. They may have landed on Staten Island.

The next explorer, who is known to have visited the area in 1525, was Estevar Gomes, who was from Portugal. After Gomes,

In the early 1600s, Samuel de Champlain explored the lake—later named for him—that separates northern New York and Vermont and helped establish French claims in the New World. *(National Archives of Canada)*

there were no known European settlements in the area for almost 100 years. There is evidence, though, that as early as 1540, French fur traders were trading along what would later be known as the Hudson River. Jacques Cartier had explored the area of the St. Lawrence River in three separate voyages, in 1534, 1535, and 1541. It was Cartier who established the French claim to Canada that overlapped the lands claimed by England in the northeastern quadrant of North America. The French set up trading posts on the St. Lawrence River at the sites of both modern-day Quebec City and Montreal.

It was 1609 before there was any more formal exploration of the area that is now New York. In that year, Samuel de Champlain traveled south from French Canada into the area that would become New York

Champlain and the Iroquois

On his expedition south along Lake Champlain and into the upper reaches of the Hudson River, Champlain traveled with a small group of French traders. They were accompanied by Native Americans from the Montagnais and Huron and from other Algonquian-speaking tribes. On the shores of Lake Champlain, this group came across a group of Iroquois. There was a long-standing rivalry between the Native Americans with Champlain and the Iroquois. When the two groups met, they fought. Champlain and his men easily defeated the Iroquois, who were still armed with traditional weapons and had never fought against people with rifles.

In part because of this battle, the Iroquois allied themselves first with the Dutch and later with the English. During the next almost 150 years, the French and Iroquois fought against each other. In the four wars that were fought between the French and English in North America, the Iroquois were one of the very few groups that fought with the English. Had Champlain been able to make allies of the Iroquois, the map of North America might look different today.

and Vermont. Champlain traveled along the lake that now bears his name and separates the two states.

While Champlain explored the northern part of the area, in 1609 the Englishman Henry Hudson sailed into the mouth of the river that today bears his name. Hudson believed that the continents of North and South America were narrow and that a passage probably existed that would make it possible to reach Asia. On his first expedition, in 1607, he sailed for the English Muscovy Company and tried to find what was called the Northwest Passage. In 1608, he tried again to find a northern passage to Asia. This time he tried to go east around the northern end of Europe. Both times, he was forced to turn back because of cold temperatures and frozen oceans.

Henry Hudson sailed the *Half Moon* in a 1609 expedition sponsored by the Dutch East India Company. Holland built this replica of the ship in 1909 and donated it to the people of New York for a celebration commemorating the 300th anniversary of Hudson's discovery of the river later named for him. This replica burned in 1931, but a newer replica built in New York was launched in 1989. *(Library of Congress, Prints and Photographs Division [LC-USZ62-72068])*

Sponsored by the English Muscovy Company, Henry Hudson completed his first expedition in search of the Northwest Passage. *(National Archives of Canada)*

Hudson was unable to find sponsorship for a third voyage in England. So he turned to the Dutch for financial backing. The Dutch East India Company agreed to outfit a ship called the *Half Moon*, and Hudson sailed to North America. He was once again in search of a northwest passage. As he sailed north into colder and colder weather, his crew mutinied and forced him to turn south. In September 1609, the *Half Moon* reached the mouth of a large navigable river.

EARLY EXPLORATION OF NEW YORK

Hudson spent over a month exploring the river and gave it his name. Hudson and his crew were able to sail the *Half Moon* almost 150 miles up the river to approximately the site of modern-day Albany, New York. During

Henry Hudson explored in 1609 what would become known as the Hudson River in present-day New York. In this reproduction of a painting, an American Indian family observes Hudson entering the river's bay. *(Library of Congress, Prints and Photographs Division [LC-USZ62-107822])*

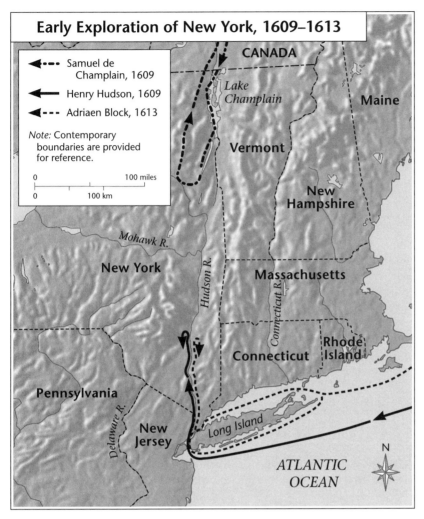

Early Exploration of New York, 1609–1613

◄ - - ▪ Samuel de Champlain, 1609

◄ ━━━ Henry Hudson, 1609

◄ - - - Adriaen Block, 1613

Note: Contemporary boundaries are provided for reference.

0   100 miles

0   100 km

CANADA

Lake Champlain

Maine

Vermont

New Hampshire

Mohawk R.

New York

Hudson R.

Massachusetts

Connecticut R.

Rhode Island

Connecticut

Pennsylvania

Delaware R.

New Jersey

Long Island

ATLANTIC OCEAN

N

While Samuel de Champlain explored New York from the north, Henry Hudson and then Adriaen Block explored the southern areas of the state.

the time Hudson and his men were on the river, they had contact with numerous Native Americans. Some they traded with and others they fought against. One group of Hudson's men were attacked by Native Americans in canoes while out exploring in one of the ship's boats. Rain made the European's rifles misfire. One of Hudson's men was shot through the neck with an arrow and died. Hudson buried him on shore at Sandy Hook.

Based on Hudson's voyage, the Dutch claimed a large slice of North America that divided the lands claimed by England. The Dutch were only able to hold the land for just over 50 years before they were forced to give it up to the English. Hudson also was forced to give into the English. On his return to Europe, he was captured by the English and had to agree that he would not sail for any country but that of his birth. His fourth and last voyage in search of a passage to Asia was once again sponsored by an English company.

One of Hudson's crew members on the *Half Moon* was Adriaen Block, who in 1613 returned to what the Dutch would call New Netherland. Block captained the ship the *Tiger* for the Dutch government. He retraced Hudson's route upriver. He sailed around Long Island, giving it its name. Block also explored the Connecticut, Rhode Island, and Massachusetts coasts. Block Island, off the coast of Rhode Island, was discovered and named by Captain Block. Block and his men almost ended up staying in New Netherland when the *Tiger* caught fire and was destroyed.

THE DUTCH WEST INDIA COMPANY

Henry Hudson was employed by the Dutch East India Company when he made the voyage that gave the Dutch a claim in North

Hudson's Fourth Voyage

When Henry Hudson returned to England after his trip to North America that was sponsored by the Dutch, he and his ships were seized by the English authorities. In exchange for his release, he agreed to serve only England in any future voyages. In 1610, a newly formed English company purchased a new ship, the *Discovery*, and hired Hudson to make another trip in search of the Northwest Passage. When he reached Hudson Strait, between the northern tip of eastern Canada and Baffin Island, it was already summer.

Hudson then spent the rest of the summer and well into the fall exploring Hudson Bay. By November, ice had begun to form in the bay, and the *Discovery* was trapped. During the winter, Hudson and his crew suffered from the cold and a lack of provisions. Being trapped on the ship caused all sorts of problems among the crew, and in June 1611 they mutinied. Hudson, his son, and seven loyal crew members were set adrift in one of the ship's boats. A few of the mutineers finally reached England, and when it was learned what had happened, they were put in prison. Henry Hudson and those who had stayed with him were never heard from again.

Block and the *Restless*

When fire destroyed the *Tiger,* Adriaen Block and his crew were able to set up camp on Manhattan Island. They spent the winter there, living in shelters they built with the help of Native Americans. Using parts salvaged from the *Tiger,* they were able to build a new ship that they named the *Restless.* They were able to safely reach home in their American-made ship, which may have been the first European-style ship built in North America.

America. The Dutch East India Company had the exclusive right to trade with the Dutch trading partners in Asia. After Hudson's voyage, there were a number of groups who sent ships to New Netherland to trade for furs with the Native Americans along the Hudson River. They did not establish any settlements and were often in competition with each other.

When the competition between traders from rival Dutch cities turned violent, the government stepped in. In 1614, a charter was issued to set up a company that had exclusive rights to the fur trade in the lands the Dutch claimed in North America. The charter gave the new company exclusive trading rights to the land bounded on the east by the Connecticut River, on the west by the Hudson, and north to the point where the Mohawk River joined the Hudson. The company was called the New Netherland Company, and its charter is the first recorded use of the name New Netherland to describe the place.

Trade continued with the Native Americans of New Netherland, and the company built a trading post near modern-day Albany. In 1621, the government in the Netherlands decided to put the private companies trading in the Western Hemisphere out of business. The government created the Dutch West India Company, which sold stock to private investors.

There were two reasons for creating the West India Company as a government-sanctioned organization. First, it would ensure that the government would profit from any trade that took place. It also gave the West India Company's ships a legitimate right to attack the shipping of the Netherlands's major rival, Spain. The plans for the West India Company were grandiose. The reality was a rather modest fleet of 20 ships that were only a minor nuisance

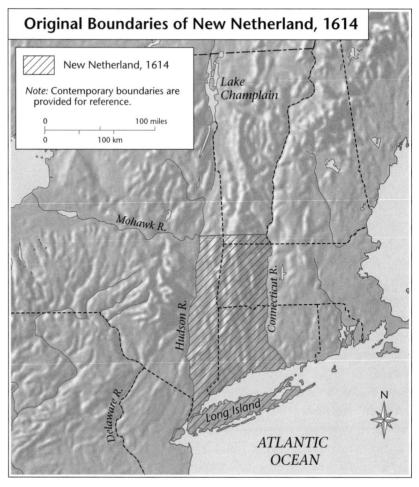

Original Boundaries of New Netherland, 1614

New Netherland, 1614

Note: Contemporary boundaries are provided for reference.

0   100 miles

0   100 km

Lake Champlain

Mohawk R.

Hudson R.

Connecticut R.

Delaware R.

Long Island

ATLANTIC OCEAN

N

The original charter of the Dutch West India Company gave them the exclusive trading rights to the land between the Hudson and Connecticut Rivers north to the mouth of the Mohawk River.

to the massive Spanish presence in Central and South America and the Caribbean.

Under the direction of the West India Company, the Native American fur trade in New Netherland was one of the few areas of profit. In 1623, they decided to establish a colony in New Netherland, where for more than 10 years they had been sending ships to trade with the Native Americans. The lower reaches of the Hudson and all of what is now known as upstate New York contained numerous Native American groups who any colonist would have to deal with.

2

The Native Americans of New York

The area that is now New York State was populated by numerous Native American groups before the coming of Europeans. Some archaeologists estimate that the first Native Americans may have been in the area as early as 11,000 years ago. These earliest Native Americans were most likely big-game hunters who lived by killing the large animals that roamed North America at the end of the last ice age. Over thousands of years, numerous Native American groups developed. Ethnographers believe that there were more than 150 different tribal groups that spoke languages that belong to as many as 60 different language families.

By the time that the first modern Europeans arrived in the area, there were approximately 10 tribes who spoke languages from two language families in the area that is now New York State. In the southeastern part of the state, there were Native Americans who belonged to five different Algonquian-speaking tribes. These tribes were the Lenni Lenape, Wappinger, Munsee, Montauk, and Mahican. In the upstate area of New York, there were also five tribes. They spoke languages from the Iroquoian language group. Before the coming of the Europeans, the Algonquian peoples were spread over more of the state, but they were forced into the lower Hudson River area by the expansion and growing power of the Iroquois.

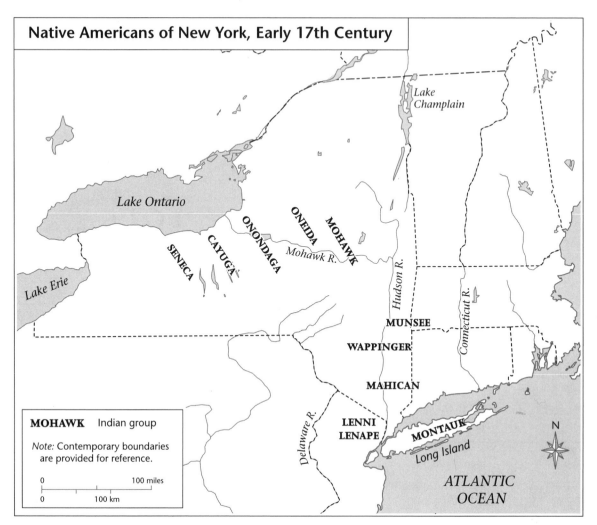

Native Americans of New York, Early 17th Century

Lake Champlain

Lake Ontario

SENECA   CAYUGA   ONONDAGA   ONEIDA   MOHAWK

Mohawk R.

Lake Erie

Hudson R.

Connecticut R.

MUNSEE

WAPPINGER

MAHICAN

Delaware R.

LENNI LENAPE

MONTAUK

Long Island

ATLANTIC OCEAN

N

MOHAWK   Indian group

Note: Contemporary boundaries are provided for reference.

0   100 miles

0   100 km

The Dutch drove out most of the Native Americans in southern New York, while the Iroquois held on to their lands throughout the colonial period.

THE LEAGUE OF THE IROQUOIS

The Iroquois, who referred to themselves as the Haudenosaune, or People of the Longhouse, were made up of five different tribes. Traveling from the Hudson River west, the five tribes were the Mohawk, the Oneida, the Onondaga, the Cayuga, and the Seneca. At some point before the coming of the Europeans, some believe as early as the 12th century, the five tribes of the Iroquois decided to stop fighting each other and join together. This group is often referred to as

Dating the Start of the League of the Iroquois

Dating events that are only recorded in the oral traditions of Native Americans is always difficult. At first, it was believed that Hiawatha helped bring peace to the People of the Longhouse sometime in the middle of the 16th century. According to oral tradition, the Seneca were the final tribe to agree to the league. The stories also claim that there was a total solar eclipse when the Seneca agreed and the league began.

Based on this fact, later historians and astronomers estimated that the league probably started in 1451, when a solar eclipse occurred. Recent research has suggested that the 1451 solar eclipse is probably not the one referred to in the stories of the league. Some scientists now believe that the 1451 eclipse would have been only a partial eclipse in central New York. They have set the date of the beginning of the League of the Iroquois to coincide with a total eclipse over central New York that occurred in 1142. This date would make the League of the Iroquois one of the oldest, continuous democracies in the world.

One of the first Iroquois rulers, Atotarho is believed to have possessed supernatural powers. In this lithograph after a drawing by Seth Eastman, he is shown (far right) with serpents growing from his head and wrapped around his body. *(Library of Congress, Prints and Photographs Division [LC-USZ62-70238])*

the League of the Iroquois. Iroquois legends give an account of the five tribes fighting each other until a prophet sent by the Great Spirit came among them calling for peace. The prophet's name was Deganawida, and he traveled in a mystical white canoe that was carved from stone. Tradition has it that he was assisted in telling the people about his call for peace by Hiawatha, a Mohawk.

The stories say that Deganawida had a powerful message to tell the people, but he stuttered and had difficulty speaking to large groups. Deganawida found Hiawatha living the life of a hermit because he had lost his family in warfare with the neighboring Onondaga. After listening to Deganawida's plan, Hiawatha, who was a strong speaker, joined him in spreading the word of peace and cooperation to the five tribes. When all the tribes agreed, it fell to the Onondaga, who lived in the middle of the league's territory, to become the keepers of the council fire. Each year, the council of the league would meet to work out any problems that had arisen between members.

Life among the Iroquois

The Iroquois tribes were part of the cultural group known as Eastern Woodlands Indians. These Indians are often divided into two "culture areas"—the Northeast and the Southeast. Prior to interference from European culture, the Iroquois lived by farming as well as hunting for meat and gathering wild plants. Everything they needed they were able to get from the forest around them. Their houses, their canoes, many of their tools and utensils, their weapons, and some of their food came from the trees of the vast forest they lived in.

A typical Iroquois village consisted of a number of longhouses built on a high point of land. The Iroquois often built a defensive wall and ditch around their towns. The ditch was usually about three feet deep. The dirt from the ditch was piled on the village side and pointed stakes were set in the dirt pile so that they leaned out over the ditch. This type of protective fence is called a palisade.

Some villages had as many as three palisades, to give the village added protection. The area inside the palisades was between five and 10 acres. The size was determined by the number of longhouses that made up the village. The smallest longhouses were about 12 feet wide and 30 feet long. The largest longhouses could

Constructing a Longhouse

To build a longhouse, the Iroquois used a large number of saplings (young trees) to make a frame. In building an average-size longhouse, the saplings were set in two rows 25 feet apart, and the rows were about 80 feet long. The saplings were then bent into the center of the row, forming an arch. Other saplings would be lashed to the arches to give the frame strength and to support the siding. The outside of a longhouse was covered with large sheets of elm bark. A second frame was constructed to hold the bark in place.

A doorway was placed in both ends of the structure, and a corridor ran down the center of the entire length of the longhouse. The longhouse was divided into apartments that were 12 to 25 feet long. A partition was built between the apartments. Along each side, inside the longhouse, a wide bench was built that was about one foot off the ground. The bench kept the inhabitants and their belongings up off the damp ground. The benches were used for sitting during the day and sleeping at night. Each apartment had a cooking fire in the center of it and two families would share each apartment, with one family on each side of the corridor.

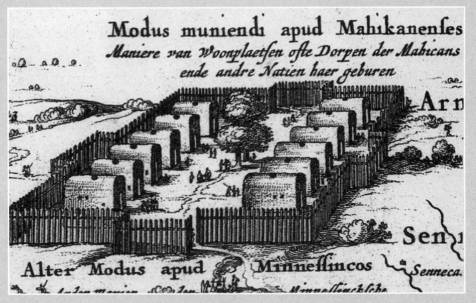

This detail of a 1685 map by Nicolaes Visscher that was based on the explorations of Henry Hudson shows longhouses, which were divided into apartments and housed many Iroquois families. *(Library of Congress)*

Native Americans used almost every part of the white-tailed deer that they killed, and the Iroquois depended heavily on them as a source of food and materials. *(National Park Service)*

be as big as 25 feet wide and 200 feet long. The average longhouse was 25 feet wide and about 80 feet long.

All the people who lived in one longhouse were related. Iroquois society was organized and based on matrilineal clan relationships. This means that when a child was born, he or she would become a member of his or her mother's clan. Young women continued to be a part of their mother's household. Young men, when they married, would go to live with their wife's family. Most Native Americans had a similar clan structure. Among the Iroquois, all five tribes were divided into a number of clans. Some of the clans were the same in all the tribes, which helped keep the people united, as it was believed that all the members of each clan shared relatives in the distant past. The clans were named after animals, such as the snipe, wolf, bear, deer, turtle, beaver, heron, hawk, and eel.

Agriculture was an important part of the life of the Iroquois. Their primary crops were corn, beans, and squash. The Iroquois referred to the spirits of these crops as the Three Sisters. They also grew smaller amounts of sunflowers for food, and tobacco to smoke as part of their religious activities.

Iroquois Footwear

The Iroquois primarily wore deerskin moccasins on their feet. Their moccasins were made from a single piece of deerskin. They would sew a seam over the toes and at the heel so the moccasins would fit snugly. The moccasins had a flap at the ankle that was usually worn down, but it could be laced up as well. Often, the Iroquois decorated their moccasins with beads and porcupine quills. Once they began trading with Europeans, they acquired additional types of beads to decorate their moccasins and clothing. In the summer, many Iroquois wore sandals made from cornhusks.

The three main crops were usually grown together. It was difficult for the Iroquois to clear the forest for fields, so it was important to use the cleared land efficiently. Corn was planted in small hills along with the beans. The two plants were beneficial to each other. The corn stalks served as supports for the beans to climb on. Beans are a legume, which means they have the ability to take nitrogen from the air and release it in the soil. Corn needs lots of nitrogen to grow. The squash was planted between the corn hills so less weeding had to be done. The women, girls, and the youngest boys did most of the work in the fields.

Native Americans were also accomplished hunters who ate the flesh of numerous fish, birds, and mammals. The most important animal to the Iroquois, and most Woodland Indians, was the white-tailed deer. Deer were an important source of meat. They were also important for many other reasons. Their bones and antlers were used to make numerous tools. Their hides were the primary source of clothing and footwear. Dresses, pants, skirts, shirts, and moccasins were all made from deerskin.

Hunting was primarily done by the men and the older boys of the village using bows and arrows. Hunting was generally done in the fall and winter. In the winter, deer come together in herds in sheltered softwood trees known as deer yards. Iroquois hunters would take advantage of this by hunting the deer in the yards. They were especially successful at this because they were able to stay on top of the deep snow using snowshoes. The Iroquois often set up temporary hunting camps far from their home villages. Generally, the women and children would also travel to the hunting camps so that the work of smoking and drying the deer meat, or venison, could be done quickly before the meat spoiled.

In addition to deer, the Iroquois hunted for moose, bear, and numerous smaller animals. They also took advantage of the abundant fish in the lakes, rivers, and streams of

The Iroquois caught many Atlantic salmon in the Hudson River each year. *(U.S. Fish and Wildlife Service)*

New York. They used bone hooks, spears, and nets to catch all sorts of fish. Much of their fishing was done in the spring, when fish would run up the streams and rivers to spawn.

The Hudson River had a huge run of Atlantic salmon each spring. The Iroquois would catch large quantities of salmon as they left the Hudson and entered the Mohawk River. One of the ways they caught fish was to build a weir in the river. A weir is a series of stone walls built out into the river that the fish were forced to swim around. At the opening in the last wall, the Iroquois would place nets to catch the fish. This technique was also used in smaller streams that ran into the many lakes in the area inhabited by the Iroquois.

The Iroquois traveled throughout what is now New York, Vermont, Pennsylvania, Ohio, and north into the area that is now the Canadian provinces of Quebec and Ontario. Throughout their home territory, there was a network of established trails. The Central Trail of the Iroquois connected the five tribes and ran from the Hudson River, near modern-day Albany, to the shores of Lake Erie near Buffalo.

They also used canoes to travel along the many lakes and rivers of their area. The Iroquois used a bark canoe similar to the birch bark canoes that many people are familiar with. However, since the birch tree was not that common in the home territory of the Iroquois, their canoes were made from elm and hickory bark. As the Iroquois traveled through this huge area, they hunted and traded with other Native American groups. Some other Native Americans did not like the Iroquois traveling into or through their territory, and there was often fighting.

Some of the tribes that the Iroquois often fought with were the Algonquian-speaking tribes who lived in the southeastern area of New York. The Algonquian tribes had once inhabited part of the territory that became the homeland of the Iroquois, and their differences went far back in time.

THE ALGONQUIAN-SPEAKING TRIBES OF NEW YORK

The Lenni Lenape, Wappinger, Munsee, Montauk, and Mahican tribes of the southeastern part of New York shared many cultural similarities with the Iroquois. They grew the same crops, hunted the same animals, gathered the same plants from the forest, built similar boats, and used similar weapons. One area where the two groups differed, other than their languages, was in the type of houses they lived in. The Algonquian tribes did not build the huge longhouses preferred by the Iroquois. They used a similar

Wampum

The Native American groups along the East Coast of North America made beads using clamshells. They used a variety of clamshells to create white beads, which were always more plentiful than the darker beads. They used the quahog clamshell to produce dark beads that ranged in color from black to purple and blue. The beads were then strung on leather or hemp twine and fashioned into belts and jewelry.

Much of the wampum was used for decoration, but some wampum belts used a series of symbols that depicted a story or sent a message from one group to another. The Native Americans who had access to the coast often traded wampum for goods with other Native Americans in the interior of the continent. Historical accounts of contacts with the Native Americans in southeastern New York indicate that they were experts at fashioning elaborate items using wampum.

The colonists soon began to use wampum as money. In the early years of the American colonies, there was little or no money available. At first, people exchanged food as a form of currency, but this had many drawbacks—the major one being its perishable nature. If not consumed, the person accepting the food would soon lose his or her profit. To solve this problem, the colonists began to accept wampum in exchange for goods, and the colonial governments set exchange rates. They also began to manufacture wampum.

In New Netherland, the exchange rate was set at four white beads equaling one stiver, the Dutch currency. The black or dark beads were worth twice as much. A stiver was the equivalent of an English pence. The last recorded use of wampum as money took place in New York in 1701.

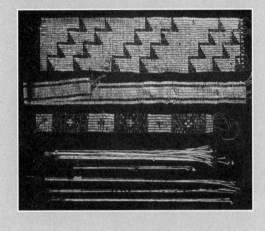

Wampum's uses ranged from recording agreements to sending messages, but its use as money became more important for tribes after the arrival of European explorers and settlers. *(National Archives, Still Picture Records, NWDNS-106-IN-18A)*

Native Americans and European Diseases

When Europeans came to North America, they brought with them numerous diseases that were common in Europe but were unknown to the Native Americans they came in contact with. Diseases such as measles, mumps, influenza, and smallpox had a devastating impact on Native Americans. Many Europeans had developed immunities to these diseases, but Native Americans had none. They often died from a disease that might make a European only mildly sick.

The most deadly of the European diseases was smallpox. It killed whole villages of Native Americans. When the Europeans learned of the effect of these diseases, a few unscrupulous people are reported to have intentionally infected groups of Native Americans by giving them blankets and/or clothing that had been used by sick Europeans. It will never be known how large the Native American population was when the first Europeans arrived. Historians do agree that a large percentage of the Native American population died from disease. Had that not happened, settlement along the East Coast by Europeans might have been very different.

technique of bark-covered frames, but they built much smaller structures that are usually called wigwams.

The tribes that lived in the coastal area ate fish and shellfish much more than the Iroquois and other inland tribes. One by-product of eating shellfish was the beads that the Native Americans made from clamshells. These beads are known as wampum, and they were an important trade good among the Native Americans of the northeastern part of North America. Wampum was used in a number of ways.

One big difference between the Iroquois and the Algonquian tribes in New York was the experience they had with Europeans. The tribes along the lower Hudson River fought numerous times with the early Dutch explorers, traders, and settlers. They also were more frequently exposed to European diseases, which had a devastating effect on the Native American population. Far more Native Americans died from European disease than died from warfare with the Dutch, English, and French. Long before the end of the colonial period, the Algonquian tribes of New York had either moved out of the area or had been wiped out.

The Iroquois, because of the strength of their society and because they became valuable trading and military partners to the colonists, were able to survive throughout the period. The furs they traded with the Dutch and later the English were an important part of the colonial economy. The Iroquois were also valuable allies during the four wars that were fought, in part, in New York against the French of Canada and their Native American allies. Today there are still large numbers of Iroquois in New York and Canada.

3

The Dutch Settle New Netherland

Shortly after Henry Hudson established a claim to New Netherland for the Dutch in 1609, traders began making annual trips to the Hudson River to trade with Native Americans for furs. After the Dutch West India Company was established in 1621, plans were made to establish permanent settlements within the area granted to the Dutch West India Company. Their grant included all the lands between the Connecticut River to the north and Delaware Bay to south. Although this land had not been settled by the English, much of the Dutch claim overlapped land also claimed by the English.

In the early part of the 17th century, England, France, Spain, Sweden, Russia, and the Netherlands all tried to stake claims in North America. In the end, it did not matter what a country claimed. What turned out to be important was the land that could be settled and held. In April 1624, the Dutch West India Company sent out the ship *Nieu Nederlandt* (*New Netherland*), which carried 30 families, many of whom were French-speaking Walloons. A little more then 100 men, women, and children arrived at the mouth of the Hudson River.

Rather than stay together and establish one colony, the company wanted to establish trading posts throughout the lands it claimed. Eighteen families were sent 150 miles up the Hudson River, where they established Fort Orange. Other families were sent to start trading posts on the Connecticut and Delaware Rivers. The

Walloons

As the Dutch West India Company was trying to establish a colony in New Netherland, the Netherlands was one of the most prosperous countries in Europe. In fact, many people, including religious dissidents from England, were moving into the Netherlands. Very few people wanted to leave. During this period, the Netherlands included the area that is now Belgium. The southern part of Belgium is mostly populated by French-speaking Catholics known as Walloons.

Some of the Walloons who had become Protestants probably experienced discrimination from their Catholic neighbors. A large percentage of the 30 families that came to New Netherland in 1624 were Walloons.

small group that stayed at the mouth of the Hudson spent their first winter on what they called Noten Island. It is now known as Governor's Island.

The scattered people of New Netherland were under the control of a single director, appointed by the company in Amsterdam. Cornelis May was the first director, but after one year he was replaced by Willem Verhulst, who arrived in 1625 with 105 head of livestock, 42 more settlers, and the engineer Cryn Fredericksen,

This detail of a 1639 map of the New York City region attributed to Joan Vinckeboons shows Manhattan Island with the North (Noort) River (present-day Hudson River) labeled alongside it. *(Library of Congress)*

who was to design a town and fort at a place that would be called new Amsterdam.

NEW AMSTERDAM

Verhulst brought the colonists who had been sent to Connecticut and Delaware back to join what would become the main settlement of the colony. In 1626, the small settlement left Noten Island and moved to the much larger island of Manhattan. Once they were on Manhattan, Fredericksen laid out a small town and a fort on the southern tip of the island. All the colonists were

The Purchase of Manhattan

A long-held story credits Peter Minuit with buying Manhattan Island for the equivalent of $24 worth of beads, blankets, and other trinkets. However, when Minuit arrived to replace Verhulst, the island had already been purchased for 60 florins' worth of goods. According to the records of the West India Company, Minuit did buy Staten Island for "duffels, kettles, axes, hoes, wampum, drilling awls, Jews harps, and diverse other small wares."

Throughout the early years of all the colonies in North America, there was an ongoing misunderstanding about property ownership between the Europeans and the Native Americans. Native Americans did not own land as European did. They saw land as something to be used and shared with the members of their tribe. It is probable that they thought they were giving the Europeans the right to use the land, not own it. This created many problems in New Netherland and elsewhere.

The stories of the Dutch's purchase of Manhattan and Staten Islands, such as that of Peter Minuit (shown here) buying Manhattan Island for 60 guilders, illustrate the difference between the Native Americans' and the colonists' understanding of ownership and land. *(Library of Congress)*

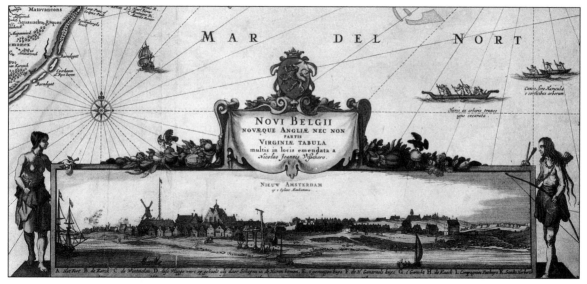

This detail of a 17th-century map of New Netherland by Nicolaes Visscher is a vignette of New Amsterdam, which would later become New York City. *(Library of Congress)*

employees of the company and were expected to do as the director ordered.

The company assumed that the colony could quickly become self-sufficient. Many of the settlers were expected to establish farms, known as "boweries" in the Dutch language. Although farms were established, they did not produce enough to feed the colony, and the company was often forced to trade for more food from local Native Americans. The company was primarily interested in making the fur trade as profitable as possible. According to the company's records, between 1624 and 1628, 31,024 beaver and 3,087 otter pelts, along with a variety of other less valuable pelts, were shipped out from New Netherland. The value of the furs shipped was reported to be more than 225,000 florins.

Charter of Freedoms and Exemptions

Despite the volume of furs, the company was showing little or no profit from New Netherland for its investors or directors. One of the directors was an Amsterdam diamond merchant named Kiliaean Van Rensselaer, who wanted to devise a system where investors would be granted large sections of the colony. The investor would become the patroon, or patron, of the lands granted and would be responsible for sending at least 50 adults to the granted lands, which were called a patroonship. After much debate between the 19 directors of the company, Van Rensselaer's plan was adopted in hopes of generating more revenue from the colony.

The new set of rules for the settlement of New Amsterdam was called the *Charter of Freedoms and Exemptions*, and they were adopted in June 1629. In addition to providing for the patroonships, the new charter also provided for much smaller grants of land. The company offered as much land as they could improve to anyone willing to come to New Netherland. Although this appeared on the surface to be a good opportunity, the rents that would be owed the company were rather steep, and very few people in the Netherlands saw any benefit to leaving their comfortable lives for the uncertainties of America.

The charter offered the patroon who was willing to sponsor the minimum of 50 colonists a huge grant of land. Because the land along the shores of New Netherland rivers was considered the most valuable, patroonships were measured in terms of shore frontage. A successful patroon could claim four leagues (12 miles) along one bank of a river. If the patroonship was to be on both

Rensselaerswyck

Van Rensselaer was ready to act as soon as the company passed the rules allowing patroonships. Van Rensselaer claimed land on both sides of the Hudson River near Fort Orange. His agent, Bastiaen Jansz Krol, negotiated for the purchase of the land from the Mahican. Van Rensselaer immediately sent tenants and managers to his private estate. The people who arrived came from all over northern Europe. There were Norwegian, Danish, German, English, and Dutch settlers who established Rensselaerswyck in 1630. There were soon farms, mills, a brewery, and a tannery in operation. At its height, Rensselaerswyck covered more than 1 million acres and was probably the largest privately owned piece of land in colonial America. The estate spanned what are now the counties of Albany, Columbia, and Rensselaer in New York. The cities of Albany and Rensselaer are both situated on lands that were part of Rensselaerswyck. The land claims of Rensselaerswyck continued into the 19th century. The last tenants rioted in 1839, and as a result, they were allowed to buy the lands they were still renting from Van Rensselaer's descendants.

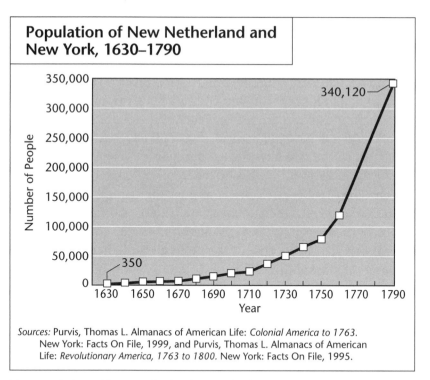

Population of New Netherland and New York, 1630–1790

350

340,120

Sources: Purvis, Thomas L. Almanacs of American Life: *Colonial America to 1763.* New York: Facts On File, 1999, and Purvis, Thomas L. Almanacs of American Life: *Revolutionary America, 1763 to 1800.* New York: Facts On File, 1995.

The population of New Netherland grew slowly. However, in the years just before and after the Revolution, New York's population expanded rapidly.

sides of the river, then the grant was for two leagues (6 miles) on both shores. There was no limit to how far from the river the patroonship covered. Five patroonships were granted by the company, but only one of them, Van Rensselaer's, was successful.

Despite the success of Rensselaerswyck, the other Dutch patroonships were failures. Michael Pauw was granted a patroonship in 1630 that he called Pavonia. It included all the land on the New Jersey shore of the Hudson from the southern tip of Staten Island, which was part of the grant, north to what is today Hoboken, New Jersey. By 1636, Pavonia had yet to provide any profits for Pauw and his partners. The patroonship was sold back to the company. The other patroonships in New York, Connecticut, and Delaware were also failures.

The 1629 charter failed to bring many more people to New Netherland. In 1630, the population of the colony was only 350 people. Ten years later, there were still fewer than 2,000 people in New Netherland. At the same time, there were almost 13,000 people in the English colonies in New England. One way the company dealt with the labor shortage in New Netherland was to import slaves.

The Dutch were more involved in the African slave trade than were any other European country. Many of the Africans who came to the Americas as slaves arrived on Dutch ships. The company, as well as individuals in New Netherland, owned slaves. It has been reported that most of the slaves who were brought to New Amsterdam had already been slaves for a while in the Dutch colonies of South America and the Caribbean. Slaves imported directly from Africa were more likely to resist their enslavement. Those who had been forced to accept their plight on large plantations were less likely to rebel.

Slavery was an accepted practice in all the American colonies. In some of the southern English colonies, slaves made up a substantial percentage of the population. By 1720, South Carolina's population was 70 percent African-American slaves. In Virginia, 30 percent of the population was slaves. In the northern colonies, slavery was not as prevalent. In 1720, the number of slaves in Massachusetts, Connecticut, and New Hampshire made up about 2 percent of the population. The use of slaves started by the Dutch continued in New York, and in 1720, African Americans, most of whom were slaves, made up 16 percent of the population.

In 1640, the company again changed its rules in hopes of attracting more settlers. The new *Charter of Freedoms and Exemptions* promised 200 acres to anyone who brought five adults to the colony. In addition, and probably even more important, was the provision that allowed these new settlements a certain amount of self-government. It was at this time that Puritans from New England began to settle on Long Island. Many of these new settlers had experienced religious conflicts in New England and wanted to be able to worship as they chose.

Although the Puritans in New England had left Britain to avoid religious persecution, they were not tolerant of people who wanted to worship differently than they did. Roger Williams founded Rhode Island because he did not agree with the church leaders in Boston. The first group of New England Puritans to settle on Long Island was a group from Lynn, Massachusetts. In June 1640, they founded the town of Southampton. In a relatively short period of time, there were Puritan settlements at East Hampton and Southold as well.

4

Life in New Netherland

THE FUR TRADE

As the colony of New Netherland slowly grew in its early years, a pattern of daily life began to evolve. The primary business of the company was the fur trade. Many of the people in the colony took part in some aspect of the trade. Although the company had a monopoly, there were a number of exceptions, as well as a certain amount of illegal trade.

The majority of the furs shipped out of New Netherland came from trade with the Iroquois. To meet the demand for furs, the Iroquois expanded their hunting area. Many times, this involved having to fight with tribes whose lands they trapped on. The Iroquois also served as middlemen, trading with distant tribes and then reselling the furs to the Dutch. Most of the Iroquois's furs went out through Fort Orange, which remained a company outpost even though it was in the middle of Rensselaerswyck.

There were also a substantial number of furs that came down the Delaware River to the Dutch and Swedish trading posts there. The Connecticut River fur trade created some problems for the Dutch. The river stretches north from Long Island Sound to what is now the border between New Hampshire and the Canadian province of Quebec. The Dutch claimed it as the eastern boundary of New Netherland and considered the furs that came down the river theirs. The English settlers of New England also wanted

A detail of a 1715 map of British possessions in North America drawn by Herman Moll. This industrious beaver colony working near Niagara Falls represents the economic possibilities and resources the colonies contained. *(Library of Congress)*

a piece of the Connecticut River fur trade, and there were numerous conflicts that eventually led to a treaty between the New England colonies and New Netherland. Individuals also tried to get in on the fur trade. Some farmers did their own trapping in the winter when the pelts were in their best condition. Others traded directly with nearby Native Americans in violation of company rules.

The primary fur traded was the pelt of the beaver. A distant second were the pelts of otters. Other pelts that were traded were mink and wildcat. By 1650, more than 45,000 pelts a year were shipped out of New Netherland. In exchange for the pelts, the Native Americans received a wide variety of trade goods.

The highest demand among the Native Americans was for objects made of metal. Iron axes, hatchets, knives, kettles, traps, nails, needles, and fishhooks soon were common goods among the Native Americans. Dutch pottery and a variety of cloths was also part of the trade. In the 1630s, the Dutch added another item to their list of trade goods. Muskets and the gunpowder and shot to go with them were soon in high demand by Native Americans. Within a short time, the Iroquois and Algonquian tribes were as well armed as the Dutch, which would soon create even more problems for the struggling colony.

GOVERNOR KIEFT AND THE NATIVE AMERICAN THREAT TO NEW NETHERLAND

In 1638, Peter Minuit was replaced by Willem Kieft as the director of New Netherland. The company felt that Kieft had the business experience to help make the colony turn a profit. He was given complete control to do whatever it took to improve the profit picture in America. Before Kieft's arrival, there had been minor conflicts between the Native Americans and the Dutch settlers. Kieft saw only one solution to the problem: The Native Americans who had not died from disease were to be wiped out by war.

First, however, Kieft decided that the Native Americans along the lower Hudson should share the burden caused by the need to maintain a military defense in the colony. On September 15, 1639, he therefore enacted a tax upon the Native Americans. The remaining Algonquians of the area objected to the idea of giving the Dutch tribute so they would be better able to attack the Native Americans.

Undaunted by the absurdity of his tax scheme, Kieft went forward with his persecution of Native Americans. In May 1640, Native Americans on Staten Island killed hogs that had wandered into their cornfield and destroyed their recently planted crops. In reaction to the killing of the hogs, Kieft did two things. First, he made a rule that any Dutch settlers who lived near Native American fields should either keep an eye on their animals or fence them in so they would not destroy the Native Americans' crops. Kieft's second action is hard to believe today.

In retribution for the killed hogs, Kieft sent out 50 soldiers and 20 sailors in summer 1640 to teach the Native Americans of Staten Island and what would be northern New Jersey a lesson. The Dutch force went on a rampage of murder and destruction. They burned Native American fields and villages. They also murdered numerous Native Americans. At one point, the Dutch threw Native American babies into the river, and then they shot the parents when they tried to save their children.

This period of genocide against the Native Americans of the lower Hudson River area is known as Kieft's War or the Pig War. The fighting between Kieft's Dutch forces and the Native Americans lasted for more than five years. By the end of it, many colonists had died and more than 1,000 Native American men, women, and children had been killed. Although there continued to be conflicts between the colonists and Native Americans along the frontier settlements, the Native Americans along the lower Hudson no longer posed a threat to the colony.

Even though Kieft's War secured the future for the colonists, he alienated many of them with his brutal and high-handed tactics. Many colonists complained bitterly to the company, and in 1647, Kieft was replaced as director of New Netherland by Peter Stuyvesant. Stuyvesant served as governor for 17 years. His tenure was the longest of any colonial governor, and he was the last Dutchman to rule New Netherland.

PETER STUYVESANT RUNS NEW NETHERLAND

The years of Kieft's War and neglect had taken their toll on New Netherland. The conditions were deplorable when Peter Stuyvesant stepped off the ship, the *Princess*, onto the docks of New Amsterdam on May 11, 1647. Stuyvesant had been employed by the West India Company for a number of years, and he had lost much of his right leg during a battle with the Spanish in the Caribbean. His wooden leg was decorated with silver. As Stuyvesant inspected the city, he saw much that needed attention. More than 1,000 people lived in New Amsterdam, and the town was a mess.

The fort was in poor repair, livestock wandered everywhere, people threw their garbage in the streets, and public drunkenness was a serious problem. Over the next few years, Stuyvesant did much to improve conditions in the colony. One of the first rules he passed was to close the taverns of the town at 9 P.M. and not let them open on Sunday until after noon. One out of every four businesses in New Amsterdam was a tavern or was a place that sold alcohol. Knife fights were a common problem among the drunken patrons of the taverns.

To help solve some of these problems, Stuyvesant instituted the first police force in the colony. It was called the "Rattle Watch" because all the nine police officers carried a large rattle as they patrolled the streets between 9 P.M. and 6 A.M. If an officer came upon a fight, he would make noise with his rattle and other officers would rush to help him.

Peter Stuyvesant became director of New Netherland in 1647. *(Delaware Public Archives)*

In addition to a police force, Stuyvesant wrote a fire code requiring people to keep their chimneys clean. He also provided fire buckets and organized the town to create bucket brigades to deal with fires when they started. Animals were fenced in, and throwing garbage in the road was punished with a fine. The residents of the town were also fond of driving their carriages at high speed through the narrow streets of the town. Stuyvesant created a rule that carts and carriages had to be walked through town except on the widest street, which became known as Broadway.

On the surface, Stuyvesant's rules seemed to have been well thought out and to the benefit of the town. However, numerous people complained both in New Amsterdam and to the company because Stuyvesant raised taxes to pay for his improvements. His rules to reduce the quantity of alcohol consumed by the

Evidence of the Dutch Reformed Church's presence in New Amsterdam can be seen in this lithograph of a Dutch church's interior in Albany. This particular church was built in 1715, after the English gained control of the colony, and demolished about a century later. *(Library of Congress, Prints and Photographs Division [HABS, NY, 1-ALB, 10-1])*

residents of the colony and sold to Native Americans had little impact. Stuyvesant even tried to put a stop to some of the illegal breweries in the colony. However, the colonists were partial to their beer, and the ordinances had little effect. In fact, a couple of years after Stuyvesant arrived, there was a bread shortage because the ample wheat harvest in the colony was being diverted by the beer makers.

Despite the grumblings of people living in the colony, there was an influx of new colonists shortly after Stuyvesant arrived. Although this was good for the colony, it pointed out some of the shortcomings of Stuyvesant and his allies among the Dutch Reformed clergy in the colony. The new arrivals came from all over Europe and brought with them numerous religious beliefs and practices. The company in Amsterdam wanted any and all newcomers to populate the colony. However, Stuyvesant and others had no toleration for anyone who believed differently than they did. Lutherans, Quakers, Puritans, and Jews all felt the director's prejudice.

Although Stuyvesant accepted the directions of the company relating to the Jews, he openly persecuted any Quakers who came into New Netherland. One Quaker who passively resisted the prejudice of Stuyvesant was publicly beaten and then banished from the colony. On December 27, 1657, a group of Quakers who lived in Flushing (now in Queens, part of modern-day New York City) were so upset by the governor's actions that they wrote a letter of protest to him. Instead of listening to their protests, Stuyvesant had a number of the signers of the letter arrested.

As the colony grew, Stuyvesant had to make other concessions to people living there. One of the changes that had taken place in the company's new rules in 1640 was the offer of limited

The First Jews in New Amsterdam

In 1492, King Ferdinand and Queen Isabella of Spain banished the large Jewish population from Spain. These Jews had been forced to leave their homes and resettle throughout Europe. A number of them ended up in the Netherlands. Some of their descendants had moved to Dutch colonies in the Caribbean and South America. When the Dutch lost their colony at Pernambuco, Brazil, in 1654, 23 Jews from there ended up in New Amsterdam.

Stuyvesant did not want to let them stay, and he wrote to Amsterdam asking that "none of the Jewish nation be permitted to infest New Netherland." The company knew it needed every possible settler if the colony was to survive the growing threat from the surrounding English colonies and refused to go along with Stuyvesant. They instructed him to allow them to remain in the colony as long as they did not openly practice their religion.

The handful of Jews in New Amsterdam secretly met to hold religious services, and the first Jewish Rosh Hashanah services in what is now the United States were held in New Amsterdam on September 12, 1654. The group of Jews in New Amsterdam was the beginning of the Congregation Shearith Israel, which is the oldest Jewish congregation in North America.

The building in this early 20th-century photograph served as a meeting house for the Society of Friends, or Quakers, near Pawling, New York. *(Library of Congress, Prints and Photographs Division [HABS-NY, 14-QUAHI, 1-])*

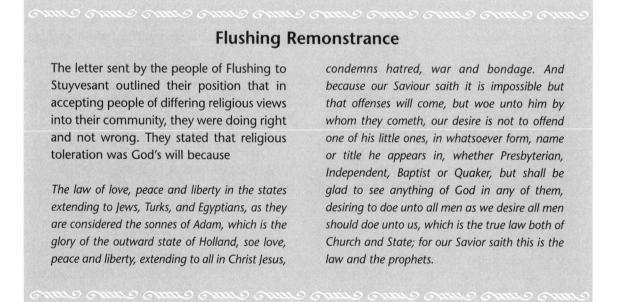

Flushing Remonstrance

The letter sent by the people of Flushing to Stuyvesant outlined their position that in accepting people of differing religious views into their community, they were doing right and not wrong. They stated that religious toleration was God's will because

The law of love, peace and liberty in the states extending to Jews, Turks, and Egyptians, as they are considered the sonnes of Adam, which is the glory of the outward state of Holland, soe love, peace and liberty, extending to all in Christ Jesus, *condemns hatred, war and bondage. And because our Saviour saith it is impossible but that offenses will come, but woe unto him by whom they cometh, our desire is not to offend one of his little ones, in whatsoever form, name or title he appears in, whether Presbyterian, Independent, Baptist or Quaker, but shall be glad to see anything of God in any of them, desiring to doe unto all men as we desire all men should doe unto us, which is the true law both of Church and State; for our Savior saith this is the law and the prophets.*

self-government to the towns of the colony. The Puritan towns of Long Island brought the New England town meeting with them. The Dutch towns had to wait for Stuyvesant to appoint local administrators, who gave the towns some control over local affairs. Starting in 1645 with Gravesend, and then moving on to Brueckelen (Brooklyn) and Hempstead in 1646, Stuyvesant gave up some of his power. Beverwyck (or Beavertown, which the English later renamed Albany) and Newtown were incorporated in 1652. Others followed but only at the urging of the company and the reluctance of Stuyvesant.

If the problems of a growing colony were not enough, Stuyvesant also had to deal with threats to the colony along the Delaware and the Connecticut. To the south, Peter Minuit returned to North America, but he was no longer in the employ of the Dutch. He had gone to Sweden and convinced the king that there was a real opportunity to create a colony in North America and get in on the lucrative fur trade. With the backing of the Swedes, Minuit established a Swedish colony in what would become Delaware in 1638. The presence of the Swedes cut into the Dutch fur trade coming out of the Delaware watershed.

The Swedes built Fort Christiana near modern-day Wilmington. In an attempt to counteract the Swedish influence in the area, Stuyvesant sent a force to the Delaware River, where they built Fort Casimir on the New Jersey side in 1651. A few years later, the Swedes retaliated by capturing Fort Casimir. When word of this reached the company in Amsterdam, they sent reinforcements to assist Stuyvesant in resolving the problem of the trespassing Swedes once and for all.

In September 1655, more than 600 men in a fleet of seven ships sailed into Delaware Bay and demanded the surrender of the Swedish forts. Stuyvesant's force was larger than the entire population of New Sweden, which quickly surrendered. Unfortunately for Stuyvesant, dealing with his neighbors to the north was not as easy.

In 1650, Stuyvesant had met with representatives of the New England colonies in Hartford, Connecticut. Although he knew he could not stop the growing expansion of New England, he tried to hold on to as much land as he could. The Hartford Treaty, which was not ratified until 1656, gave the English colonies half of Long Island and the lands west of the Connecticut River, which were already settled by English colonists. Stuyvesant was probably relieved that he did not lose more. Later, in 1663, Stuyvesant tried to renew the Hartford Treaty to save his colony, but the end of Dutch rule in North America was only a year away, and Governor Winthrop in Boston would not deal with Stuyvesant.

As the period of Dutch rule was nearing an end, New Netherland had become a fairly prosperous and settled place. Although a large percentage of the settlers in the colony were not Dutch, the colony had adopted much from Dutch culture. Architecture, farming practices, holidays, family structure, and even simple things like games and sports had a decidedly Dutch flavor.

Most of the houses in the colony were modeled after Dutch houses in the Netherlands. The roofs were more steeply pitched than English-style houses, and the gable end of the house faced the

Built in 1734, this Dutch barn in Montgomery County, New York, shown in a 1937 photograph, has the divided doors typical of Dutch farmhouses and is held together by wooden pegs. *(Library of Congress, Prints and Photographs Division [HABS-NY, 29-FORHU, 1-1])*

Nine Pins

Bowling in a variety of forms is an ancient sport that can be traced back to the time of the pyramids in ancient Egypt. The version of bowling that the Dutch brought to New Netherland was called nine pins. Nine slender pins were arranged in a diamond pattern and the point was to knock down a certain number of them with a wooden ball. The Dutch colonists spent so much time gambling on nine pins that the colonial authorities made nine pins illegal on Sundays and holidays.

Not willing to give up their game even for a day, the residents of New Amsterdam added a tenth pin and continued to play. The bowling that is so popular today uses the 10 pins of the Dutch in New Amsterdam. Their bowling green still exists as a small park in Lower Manhattan. The park was paved over when the subway was built, but it is still called Bowling Green Park.

street. Dutch settlers frequently put large iron numbers on their houses that indicated the year it was built. Another feature of Dutch farmhouses that was common in New Netherland was a door that was split in the middle. This was so people inside could open the top half and see outside without letting the animals out. Some of the farm animals were often kept in the house, where they were safe from predators.

Many of the farms of New Netherland were very successful. The number of domestic animals, such as pigs, cattle, chickens, and horses, in the colony grew rapidly. Much of the year, the larger animals were allowed to roam loose in the woods near the farms. Hay was cut in the many salt marshes along the bays and rivers. In their fields, the Dutch settlers grew a wide variety of crops. They had learned to grow corn, beans, and squash from Native Americans. They also grew numerous crops they had brought with them, especially wheat. They also planted orchards of cherry, plum, peach, and apple trees. The area of the lower Hudson River had some of the mildest weather in the Northeast because of the warming effects of all the water in the area, and most crops did very well.

The Dutch settlers also brought their own forms of recreation with them. In the winter, they skated on the frozen ponds, went sledding, and hitched their horses to sleighs. They also brought with them a game known as "kolven," which involved hitting a ball across the ice or grass toward a stick or goal. When this game was adopted by other colonists, it evolved into three games that are

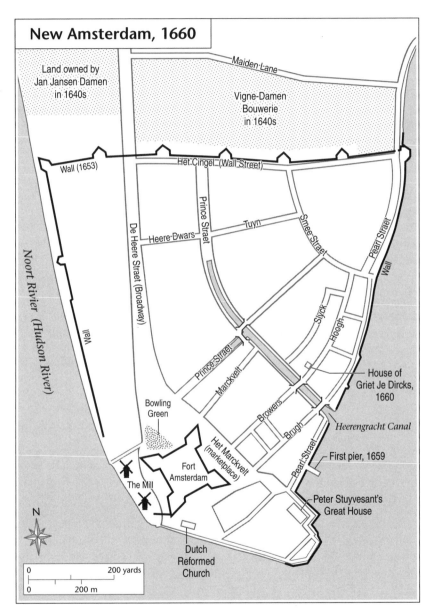

New Amsterdam, 1660

Land owned by Jan Jansen Damen in 1640s

Vigne-Damen Bouwerie in 1640s

Maiden Lane

Wall (1653)

Het Cingel (Wall Street)

Prince Straet

Tuyn

Smee Straet

Pearl Straet

De Heere Straet (Broadway)

Heere Dwars

Wall

Noort Rivier (Hudson River)

Wall

Slyck

Hoogh

Prince Straet

Marckvelt

Browers

Brugh

House of Griet Je Dircks, 1660

Bowling Green

Het Marckvelt (marketplace)

Heerengracht Canal

Pearl Straet

First pier, 1659

Fort Amsterdam

The Mill

Peter Stuyvesant's Great House

N

Dutch Reformed Church

| 0 | | 200 yards |
| 0 | 200 m | |

Although Manhattan has grown into one of the largest cities in the world, some of the original Dutch features, such as the Bowling Green found on this map, still exist in modern Manhattan.

still played today: golf, ice hockey, and field hockey. The Dutch colonists were also very fond of bowling. Very early, a bowling green was set up in New Amsterdam.

There were other differences between New Netherland and its neighboring English colonies. Among these were the attitudes toward women and children. In the Puritan colonies of New England, children were treated harshly as small adults, and only boys went to school. In New Netherland, the attitude was much different. Children were nurtured and boys and girls were both given an equal opportunity to receive schooling. Parents in New Netherland also kept their families together longer. Children who were apprenticed out to learn a trade were likely to continue to live at home. In the English colonies, apprentices usually lived with their employers.

Women also had more rights in New Netherland. They were allowed to own property, and many ended up operating family businesses after their husbands died. There are records of women in New Netherland running taverns and hotels. Others were successful fur traders. Still others were lawyers.

Although New Netherland lasted for less then 50 years, the impact of the Dutch on the area continued throughout the colonial period and beyond. When one considers the relatively small size of the colony, it is amazing how much of a contribution the Dutch made to the area that would become the United States.

5

New Netherland Becomes New York

During the 1640s, Oliver Cromwell led the Puritan forces in a civil war in England. When his forces were victorious in 1649, they removed King Charles I from the throne of England and executed him. Charles I's two sons, Charles and James, were forced to flee the country. For more than 10 years, Cromwell and his Puritan followers ruled England without a king. After Cromwell died on September 3, 1658, his son Richard took charge of the government. He was not as strong a leader as his father, and royalist forces saw the opportunity to restore the monarchy.

Charles was the older of Charles I's two sons, and he was waiting in poverty and exile in Europe for the opportunity to return to his birthright. In February 1660, royalist forces marched into London and reclaimed the government for Charles. On May 8, 1660, Parliament declared him Charles II, king of England. A little more than two weeks later, Charles II returned to England and took the throne. His brother, James, and many other loyal supporters returned to England as well. One of the many problems that faced Charles as he reasserted royal control over the British Empire was a lack of funds for himself, his supporters, and the government.

At this time, some of his advisers suggested that the North American colonies could be a source of income for the king and his most loyal supporters. First among those was his brother, James, duke of York and Albany. To reward his brother, Charles II decided to give James a large tract of land in North America. The charter outlined the lands granted to the duke. It included part of Maine extending north to the St. Lawrence River, all the islands along the coast from Cape May to Cape Cod (except Block Island), land along the western side of the Delaware River that would become Delaware and Pennsylvania, and all the land between the Delaware and Connecticut Rivers.

There were a number of problems with the lands Charles II had granted to his brother. First, they were spread out over a vast area. More important, the largest section of the grant consisted of the Dutch colony of New Netherland. The Dutch and the English had a history of poor relations. They had already fought a war in the early 1650s over trading rights around the world. When he received the charter for his lands in North America from his brother, James began to make plans to take over New Netherland.

Charles II ruled England, Scotland, and Ireland from 1660 until his death in 1685. *(Library of Congress, Prints and Photographs Division [LC-USZ62-96910])*

THE CONQUEST OF NEW NETHERLAND

Many in England believed the Dutch claim in North America was invalid. They felt that John Cabot's voyage in 1497 gave them exclusive rights to the continent. They also argued that Henry Hudson was an Englishman and could not make claims for the Dutch. Had New Netherland had as many people as Virginia or the New England colonies, the English may not have been as willing to attack it.

James used his position as the head of the British navy to send a fleet of ships to New Amsterdam under the command of Colonel Richard Nicolls. Nicolls had been in exile with many of the royalists, and he had served with James in the French army. In spring 1664, Nicolls prepared his fleet in the English town of Portsmouth. On May 14, 1664, Nicolls set sail with four ships and approximately 300 soldiers.

James, Duke of York and Albany, Later King James II
(1633–1701)

In 1649, King Charles I was removed from the throne and executed after a Puritan revolution in England. His two sons, Charles, prince of Wales, and James, duke of York and Albany, were forced to spend the next 10 years living in exile while the Puritan Oliver Cromwell ran England. Charles lived in poverty in the Netherlands, and James went to Spain, where he joined the Spanish navy in its war against Protestant England. He also fought in the French army for a short period of time. When the English monarchy was restored in 1660, James's older brother became Charles II, king of England.

Charles II appointed James lord high admiral of the navy and in 1664 granted James lands in North America. In 1672, James created a controversy by revealing that he had converted to Catholicism. Although England tolerated many different Protestant sects, the country was not tolerant of Catholics. In fact, in 1673, Parliament passed a series of laws called the Tests Acts, which barred Catholics from holding office. As a result, James was forced to resign his position as lord high admiral.

Because his brother had not produced an heir, James was next in line to become king of England. On his brother's death in 1685, many tried to block James from becoming king. However, they were unsuccessful and he became James II, king of England.

As king, he was faced with a number of uprisings in England. He was extremely brutal in addressing any resistance to his rule. He was so unpopular that in 1688, he was removed from the throne in a bloodless coup known as the Glorious Revolution. After a brief and unsuccessful attempt to regain his throne, he spent the rest of his life living in exile in France.

Nicolls sailed first to New England, where he sent word to the English settlers on Long Island, seeking their support for unseating Stuyvesant and the Dutch administration of New Netherland. Long Island and other English settlements near New Amsterdam had long been part of a tug of war between the Dutch and the Puritans in Connecticut. Five hundred militiamen were soon headed to the English settlement at Gravesend on Long Island.

On August 26, 1664, Nicolls sailed his fleet past Coney Island and dropped anchor in Gravesend Bay. Peter Stuyvesant sent a messenger out to the ships demanding to know their business. Nicolls's reply shocked the governor. When he was told that he was expected to surrender New Netherland to the British, Stuyvesant wanted to fight.

New Amsterdam was ill-prepared to defend itself. There were only about 100 professional soldiers in town, and there was a shortage of gunpowder for the big cannons of the fort. Stuyvesant sent a second messenger, who was instructed to remind Nicolls of the legitimacy of the Dutch claim to the colony. Nicolls's only reply was that Stuyvesant had 48 hours to surrender before the British and their colonial allies would attack.

The people of New Amsterdam were not as willing as their governor was to fight the British. They were especially concerned about the colonial militia from Long Island. There were already bad feelings between the two groups, and the residents of New Amsterdam feared the militia would ransack their homes and their town. Stuyvesant was adamant. He was going to fight and would have fired on the English ships that had moved into range of the fort on Manhattan had he not received a petition from the people in the town. Nicolls had made it known that the British intended to let the people of New Netherland keep their homes and businesses. Ninety-three of the city's most influential people had signed the petition, including Stuyvesant's 17-year-old son.

Faced with the military superiority of the British and the reluctance of his own people to fight, Governor Stuyvesant ran a white flag of surrender up the fort's flagpole. Over the next two weeks, Stuyvesant and Nicolls negotiated the terms of the surrender. Governor Winthrop from Connecticut served as the go-between. On September 8, 1664, the agreement was signed, and Stuyvesant and the Dutch troops in the colony marched out of the fort and boarded a ship bound for the Netherlands. Nicolls and his men landed, marched to the fort, and raised the British flag.

Nicolls proclaimed the colony part of the British Empire and named it New York after his patron. New Amsterdam became New York City, and Beverwyck, which was the major town upriver near Fort Orange, became Albany, after the duke's other title. Nicolls became governor and true to his word allowed the Dutch colonists to continue life much as they had for the last 17 years under the rule of Peter Stuyvesant. Nicolls's first order of business was to create a set of rules for governing the colony. The charter from Charles II gave the duke absolute control of the colony as long as he did not break any English laws.

Nicolls had three very different groups to deal with: the English settlements in the area, the Dutch colonists in and around

Peter Stuyvesant governed the Dutch colony of New Amsterdam (later New York City) until his surrender on September 8, 1664, to an English force led by Colonel Richard Nicolls. *(Library of Congress, Prints and Photographs Division [LC-USZ62-84401])*

New Amsterdam, and the people living upriver and on their own along the Hudson River valley. He came up with a different set of rules for each. The 17 predominantly English towns in the colony sent representatives to a meeting with Nicolls where they were asked to agree to a set of rules known as the Duke's Laws of 1665.

Nicolls had drawn up the Duke's Laws based on English common law, the practices then in place in English colonies, and certain aspects of the Dutch laws used in the colony. The one aspect missing from the Duke's Laws was any form of representative government. Historians have speculated that this was done intention-ally, to make sure the Dutch majority in the colony did not take control away from the English. Others have suggested that the duke was not interested in any representative form of government in his colony. The English settlers on Long Island were extremely upset by

The Division of the Duke's Grant

Before Nicolls had finished coming to terms with Stuyvesant, James, duke of York and Albany, had already begun dividing up the land Charles II had granted him. In 1655, two of his brother's staunchest supporters, Sir George Carteret and John, Lord Berkeley, were given the land between the Hudson and the Delaware Rivers. They named their colony New Jersey after the island of Jersey in the English Channel, where Carteret was from. The land to the west of the Delaware River eventually became the colonies of Pennsylvania and Delaware. The land claimed by Connecticut west of the Connecticut River was returned to that colony in 1667. Nantucket and Martha's Vineyard, as well as Maine, eventually ended up as part of Massachu-setts. What Nicolls was left with is the stretch of modern New York from the eastern tip of Long Island up the Hudson River to Albany, plus a large and unde-fined wilderness that was home to the Iro-quois and marauding French Canadians and their Native American allies.

Nephew of George Carteret, coproprietor of New Jersey with Lord John Berkeley, Philip Carteret (represented here) arrived in the colony as its first governor in 1665. *(Library of Congress)*

this. They had assumed that they would get the same form of representative government that was granted to the New England colonies they had come from.

Nicolls also followed through on his promise to the Dutch settlers in other ways. He guaranteed religious freedom for the colony. Although the Dutch settlers got to keep their land, they were upset by the transferring of deeds. Nicolls declared all land grants in the colony invalid until there was a new survey of the land and the new deed was registered with the British authorities. No one really lost their land, but they resented having to pay the fees Nicolls required to reregister their claims.

THE RETURN OF THE DUTCH

In 1672, Britain and the Dutch started their third and final war over control of international trade. The two nations were direct competitors from Asia to Africa to the Americas. At the time, the maritime power of Britain was still growing, while the Dutch power and influence was on the decline. On July 30, 1673, history repeated itself, only in reverse. A Dutch fleet under the command of Admiral Evertsen sailed into New York harbor and demanded the surrender of the colony. Unable to defend New York against the Dutch fleet, the colony gave up without a fight.

The Dutch flag once again flew over the island of Manhattan. The Dutch had control of the colony for only a short period of time. In 1674, a peace treaty between the British and the Dutch gave New York back to the British, and the Dutch agreed to give up any future claims in North America. Sir Edmund Andros, another royalist supporter of Charles II and James, was sent out as governor to reestablish English rule in the colony.

GOVERNOR EDMUND ANDROS

To many residents of New York, Sir Edmund Andros was the English version of Peter Stuyvesant. Andros arrived with 100 soldiers and no toleration for discussion or dissent about his leadership. His first order of business was to require every resident of the colony to swear an oath of allegiance to the Crown. When a group of eight prominent New York City Dutch leaders came to ask for

In addition to dealing with Sir Edmund Andros's harsh rule, the colonists near Albany were attacked by American Indians during King Philip's War. This engraving, published in *Harper's Magazine* in 1857, depicts the attack with great sympathy for the colonists. *(Library of Congress, Prints and Photographs Division [LC-USZ62-97113])*

assurances from the new governor that taking the oath would not affect the rights they had come to appreciate, Andros dragged them into court.

One of the eight quickly took the oath and was set free. The other seven were brought before a jury of 12 Englishmen. They were found guilty of trying to start a rebellion and were threatened with the loss of all their property. Nicholas Bayard, Stuyvesant's nephew, protested the treatment of the seven and was thrown in solitary confinement for two days. Faced with the possibility of losing everything they had, the seven men gave in and took the oath. The court reduced their fines to one-third of all their property.

**Preamble to the *Charter of
Liberties and Privileges,* 1683**

*FOR The better Establishing the Government of this province of New
Yorke and that Justice and Right may be Equally done to all persons
within the same Be It Enacted by the Governour Councell and Representatives now in General Assembly met and assembled and by the
authority of the same.*

The Dutch people of the colony were outraged but felt power-
less against Andros and his English supporters. Nicolls and the
other English governors had tread softly, leaving the Dutch to continue much as they had before 1664. Andros imposed numerous
unpopular trade and civil regulations on the colony. The cries of
protest from the colony to England forced James to recall Andros
in 1681.

He sent out another loyal supporter, Colonel Thomas Dongan,
in 1683. James was concerned that Andros's heavy-handed tactics
had brought the colony to the edge of rebellion. He instructed
Dongan to set up a colonial assembly that would be able to pass
laws. Anything passed by the Assembly was subject to the approval
of the governor and his appointed council, and by the duke.

For the people of New York, the establishment of a colonial
assembly must have been a hopeful sign. They were now on an
equal footing with the other English colonies. However, any reasons they might have had for optimism were short-lived. Charles
II died on February 6, 1785. Despite the attempts to prevent England from having a Catholic king, James succeeded his brother
and became King James II.

JAMES II AND
THE DOMINION OF NEW ENGLAND

James II was an unpopular king who went after his enemies in
England ruthlessly. He was not in favor of any form of democ-
racy and quickly asserted his control over the troublesome

Dominion of New England, 1686–1689

NEW FRANCE

St. Lawrence R.

Lake Ontario

Maine (part of Mass.)

Hudson R.

Connecticut R.

Massachusetts

Boston *Massachusetts Bay*

New York

Connecticut

Rhode Island

Plymouth

Pennsylvania

Delaware R.

New York

East Jersey

Philadelphia

West Jersey

Maryland

Delaware

Virginia

ATLANTIC OCEAN

N

| | Dominion of New England |
| | Other British colonies |

0   100 miles

0   100 km

James II made New York a part of the Dominion of New England to consolidate his control over the colonies. The dominion ended when James II was dethroned during the Glorious Revolution.

James II, as shown in this early 19th-century engraving, ruled England for only four years. *(Library of Congress, Prints and Photographs Division [LC-USZ62-92123])*

colonies in North America. His first act was to revoke the charters of all the colonies in the Northeast and combine them into what was called the Dominion of New England. The dominion included the land from Maine, New Hampshire, Massachusetts Bay, Plymouth, Rhode Island, Connecticut, New York, and New Jersey. If this was not bad enough, he sent Edmund Andros back to be governor of the dominion.

The dominion meant the end to much of the self-government that colonists had come to expect. Andros was as unpopular in the colonies as James II was in England. In London, those opposed to James II banded together to remove him from the throne. They supported his daughter Mary and her Dutch husband, William of Orange, to replace James II. When the English army threw their support behind William and Mary, James II was forced to give up his throne. This is referred to as "the Glorious Revolution" because there was no fighting.

When word reached the colonies in 1689 that James II had left the throne and was in exile in France, people rejoiced. At the time, Edmund Andros was away from Boston, which he was using as the capital of the dominion. He was on the frontier fighting against Native Americans who had been raiding English settlements. When he returned to Boston, the leaders of the town arrested him and soon sent him back to England.

William and Mary began the process of reorganizing the dominion into a number of separate colonies. Massachusetts Bay, Plymouth, and Maine were combined into the royal colony of Massachusetts. New Hampshire, Connecticut, Rhode Island, New York, and New Jersey were all granted new charters. With James II and his henchman Edmund Andros gone, many hoped the colonies could get back to business.

6

Life in
Colonial New York

In the late 17th century, New York had the most diverse population of any of the 13 English colonies. As New Netherland, the colony had attracted settlers from all over northern Europe, as well as numerous Dutch people. Long Island was mainly settled by Puritans from New England. As an English colony, New York had difficulty attracting new settlers. People coming from England chose to go to the unsettled lands in New Jersey and Pennsylvania rather than compete for land with the people already in New York. By 1690, Philadelphia had more people than the much older New York City.

Some new settlers did come to New York. French Protestants, known as Huguenots, came to New York, as well as other colonies, to escape religious persecution in France. A number of people from Scotland also settled in New York. Some people also left at this time. Some of the original settlers in New Jersey were Puritans from Long Island. During this time, New York remained one of the smaller colonies in North America. Boston was the largest and most important port in North America, while southern colonies like Virginia and Maryland were the most successful farming areas.

During much of the colonial period, New York grew slowly and remained huddled around the Hudson River and the islands at the mouth of the river. Manhattan, Staten Island, and Long Island were the centers of population in the colony. The settlements between New York City and Albany were mostly small farming communities that depended on the river for trade and communication with the rest of the colony. There were very few roads in the colony at this time. What roads there were ran from the villages to the nearest navigable waterways. North and west of Albany were the lands of the Iroquois and other Native American tribes. The Iroquois served as a buffer between the French in Canada and the English colonies. This part of New York was fought over in four wars between the French and their Native American allies and the English. The first of these wars started in 1689 and the fourth ended in 1763.

LEISLER'S REBELLION

The Glorious Revolution in England was seen as a signal to many in the American colonies that they should also rebel against King James and his supporters. Edmund Andros was arrested in Boston, which left Lieutenant Governor Nicholson in charge of New York. Nicholson, like the deposed king, James II, was a Catholic. Many of the conservative Protestants in New York and other colonies disliked the Catholic religion and discriminated against Catholics. With the fall of James II, many feared that his Catholic supporters would try to return James to the throne.

Jacob Leisler
(1640–1691)

Jacob Leisler was born in Frankfurt, Germany, in 1640 and came to New Netherland in 1660 as a soldier for the Dutch West India Company. Leisler became a trader in New Amsterdam with some success. He then married a wealthy widow, who was part of the Dutch elite in the colony. With his wife's connections and capital, Leisler quickly became one of the most successful merchants in New Amsterdam. At the time he became lieutenant governor, he was the second wealthiest man in the colony.

In addition to his wealth, Leisler was also known for his religious conservativism. His hatred of Catholics was well documented. He also found many Protestant sects too liberal, and he was a strict Calvinist. It was his religious beliefs that spurred him to lead the rebellion against Nicholson.

In New York, numerous rumors circulated about Nicholson. One rumor falsely accused him of plotting with the French Catholics to the north. The various militia groups in New York took to the streets in hopes of preventing any Catholic plots. On May 31, 1689, Nicholson argued with the militia in New York City and threatened to call out his English soldiers. Before he could do this, the militia took over the city's main fort. The militia said they would hold the city until William and Mary sent out a new Protestant governor for the colony. Nicholson returned to England intending to make a case against the colonists before the king and queen.

On June 8, 1689, the militia in control of New York City elected one of their captains, Jacob Leisler, as their leader. From his base of support among the militia, Leisler assumed the role of lieutenant governor. As lieutenant governor, Leisler expanded the right to vote to more people and was concerned about the colony's security.

In February 1690, 62 people were killed by the French and their Native American allies in Schenectady, New York. The attack

This engraving illustrates the 1690 French and Native American attack against Schenectady, New York, in which 62 colonists were killed. *(Library of Congress, Prints and Photographs Division [LC-USZ62-86415])*

helped unify New York behind Leisler as he worked to build up the defense of the colony. Leisler believed that the colonies of the Northeast needed to work together to protect themselves from the French. Leisler called for a conference in New York City, and representatives from Massachusetts, Plymouth, and Connecticut came to discuss the defense of the colonies. Connecticut even sent troops to help defend New York. Although little came from Leisler's meeting, it was an early example of the colonies trying to work together for their common good.

As lieutenant governor, Leisler became more and more dictatorial. He put some of his critics in jail. Others were forced to leave the colony. King William appointed a new governor and lieutenant governor in 1690. In January 1691, Major Richard Ingoldsby arrived in the colony as the new lieutenant governor. Leisler refused to turn over the colony, and a battle took place in New York City. When the new governor, Henry Sloughter, arrived, Leisler surrendered the city to him.

Leisler and 36 of his followers were arrested and charged with murder and treason. In March 1691, Leisler and his son-in-law, Jacob Milborne, were tried and found guilty. They were sentenced to be hanged and drawn and quartered (the body was dragged and then cut up). The sentence was carried out on May 16, 1691, and the colony of New York was once again under royal control.

Historians have argued over the impact of what is called Leisler's Rebellion. Some want to see it as one of the first acts of American rebellion. Others talk about it in terms of the religious frictions present in the colonies. Leisler turned out to be a poor leader, but he showed people in both England and the colonies that it was possible for colonists to take care of themselves. It was a precedent that would take another 85 years to turn into a full-blown revolution.

BECOMING ENGLISH

After the Leisler Rebellion, New York saw a number of royal governors come and go. Some did a good job of leading the colony, while others used their position to help themselves and their friends. One goal of all the governors of New York in the last years of the 17th century and into the 18th century was to make New York more English. Although New Netherland had been settled

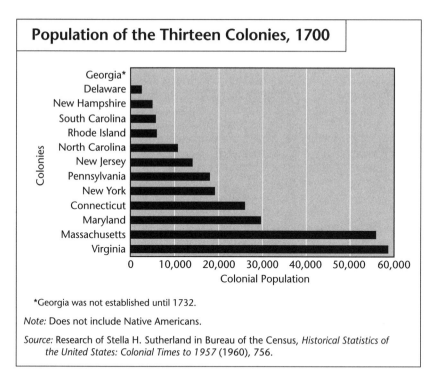

Population of the Thirteen Colonies, 1700

Colonies (top to bottom): Georgia*, Delaware, New Hampshire, South Carolina, Rhode Island, North Carolina, New Jersey, Pennsylvania, New York, Connecticut, Maryland, Massachusetts, Virginia

Colonial Population: 0, 10,000, 20,000, 30,000, 40,000, 50,000, 60,000

*Georgia was not established until 1732.

Note: Does not include Native Americans.

Source: Research of Stella H. Sutherland in Bureau of the Census, *Historical Statistics of the United States: Colonial Times to 1957* (1960), 756.

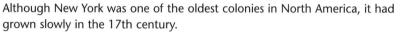

Although New York was one of the oldest colonies in North America, it had grown slowly in the 17th century.

very early, it had not grown like many of the other colonies. In 1700, New York's population made it the fifth-largest colony. However, it would soon be surpassed by Pennsylvania. New Jersey, which had been settled only since it became an English colony, in 1664, was growing much more rapidly.

There were a number of reasons for New York's slow growth. Part of the problem was the land situation. In New York, much of the best farmland was already taken by large landowners. Unfortunately, this situation was made even worse by some of the royal governors who used their position to make additional large land grants. Governor Benjamin Fletcher, who governed from 1692 to 1697, accepted large bribes from a number of wealthy New Yorkers in exchange for large grants of land throughout the colony. He also put much of the money collected by the customs officers into his own accounts. In addition, Fletcher also encouraged pirates to trade in New York.

Piracy was a serious problem during this time. When England was at war with France, many ship owners became privateers. This meant they were licensed by the Crown to attack the shipping of their enemies. When the war ended, many of these privateers continued to attack merchant ships and became pirates. Many of these pirates brought their stolen booty into New York and sold it at prices well below the goods' real market value. This enabled the merchants of New York to sell the stolen goods cheaply to their customers and still make a profit. While Governor Fletcher had encouraged this trade with pirates, his successor would try to deal with the problem.

Just before coming to New York as governor, Richard Coote, Lord Bellomont, met William Kidd, a New York ship captain who had achieved some success as a privateer. Lord Bellomont and other officials in England outfitted Captain Kidd with a new ship and asked him to sail to the west coast of Africa, where pirates based in Madagascar were attacking English merchant ships. However, like many privateers, Kidd and his crew crossed the line and were accused of piracy.

Although Governor Fletcher had supported piracy, he also worked toward making New York more English. One of his major contributions in this regard was the appointment of William Bradford as the colony's printer in 1693. Bradford became the first printer in New York. In addition to publishing the official reports of the government, Bradford published numerous pamphlets and booklets. Among his publications were two primers in English. A primer is a book intended to teach the rules of spelling, grammar, reading, and writing. These books are credited with helping the colony become more literate and with playing a part in more and more people giving up the Dutch language.

In addition to having the official proceedings of the colony published in English, changes were made in the basic

William Bradford was one of the few successful printers established in the colonies. *(Library of Congress, Prints and Photographs Division [LC-USZ62-115779])*

William Kidd
(ca. 1645–1701)

William Kidd was born in Greenock, Scotland, around 1645. He became a sailor, and sometime in the late 1680s, Kidd settled in New York. In New York, he became successful as a ship owner and sea captain. In 1695, Kidd took on the job as captain of the ship *Adventure Galley,* which had 30 guns and was designed to be a privateer. He and his crew were successful in capturing French merchant ships.

At one point, Kidd's ship was stopped by a British naval ship, and some of his crew were taken to be in the navy. This was a common and legal practice, and many British naval seamen were impressed into the service this way. To replenish his crew, Captain Kidd sailed back to New York, where he took on some new crew members. After this time, it was reported that Captain Kidd had become a pirate. In 1699, a warrant was issued for his arrest.

When the captain learned of this, he thought he had been falsely accused and sailed back to New York. Before he reached New York, he buried treasure on Gardiner's Island. Governor Richard Coote, Lord Bellomont, did not believe Captain Kidd's story that his crew had forced him to attack the wrong ships and that he had to kill one of his crew who was leading a mutiny. Lord Bellomont sent him to England to stand trial.

In London, Captain Kidd was not allowed a lawyer to help in his defense, and he was convicted of piracy and murder. Captain William Kidd was hanged on May 23, 1701,

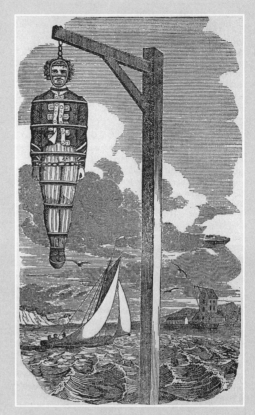

William Kidd was hanged in London on May 23, 1701. This illustration of his death appeared in an early 20th-century book about pirates. *(Library of Congress, Prints and Photographs Division [LC-USZ62-95356])*

in London. His treasure on Gardiner's Island was dug up. However, rumors existed that he had buried more treasure somewhere along the coast between Delaware and New England. Although no additional treasure was ever found, many have looked.

William Bradford
(1663–1752)

William Bradford was born in England in 1663, and he came to Philadelphia in 1682. In 1685, he started the first printing press in Pennsylvania. In 1690, he and a group of partners built the first paper mill in America, on the Schuylkill River. In 1692, he was forced to leave Pennsylvania because he printed the work of George Keith, a Scottish missionary, whose beliefs the Quaker leaders of Philadelphia disagreed with. As a result, Bradford's press was confiscated. It was after this event that he moved to New York, where he was the colony's official printer for 50 years.

In 1725, Bradford published New York's first newspaper, the *New York Gazette.* It was the official newspaper for the colony. It was Bradford's apprentice John Peter Zenger who later started the independent *New York Weekly Journal,* which criticized the government.

Edward Hyde served as governor of New York shortly after the English gained control of the colony from the Dutch. *(Library of Congress, Prints and Photographs Division [LC-USZ62-121992])*

social structures of the colony. The Dutch laws and courts were replaced by the laws of England and a court system to go along with it. The Dutch Reformed Church had been the official church of New Netherland and had received financial support from the government. Although there were very few Anglican churches in the colony, the Church of England became the official colonial church of New York.

One of the most colorful governors of this time in New York was Edward Hyde, Lord Cornbury. He was a cousin to Queen Anne and was reported to often dress like her. The religious conservatives of New York and New Jersey, where he was also governor, found it hard to accept a leader who dressed up at times like a woman. Even harder for them to accept was the governor's attempts to force Anglican priests into all the churches of the colony.

Lord Cornbury is reported to have said that the Dutch New Yorkers would never be good Englishmen as long as they had their own churches and schools. To solve this problem, he tried to get the colonial assembly to build public English schools throughout the colony. Although the assembly refused to build schools everywhere they were needed, they did vote to set up a free public school in New York City.

In many of his other dealings, Lord Cornbury was much more interested in financial gain for himself and his followers. When conflicts arose in New Jersey and New York, the governor could be counted on to support the side that offered him the largest bribe. He was even reported to have switched sides when offered a second larger bribe by the group he had at first opposed. Even Queen Anne is reported to have said, before she recalled him to England, that even though he was closely related to her, he should not be protected "in oppressing her subjects."

FREEDOM OF THE PRESS

In 1732, the former British naval admiral, William Cosby, was appointed royal governor of New York. The governorship was considered a lucrative post, and Cosby had many influential friends and relatives in England who helped him get the job. From his first arrival, it was obvious that he intended to force his will on the assembly and people of New York for his personal gain. The assembly split into two groups. The Court party supported the governor and benefited from his authority. The other group was led by Lewis Morris and was known as the country party.

In an attempt to publicize their conflict with the governor, Morris, along with James Alexander and William Smith, Jr., established a rival newspaper to publish articles critical of the governor. The paper was printed in the shop of John Peter Zenger, who had been the apprentice of the colony's official printer, William Bradford. In 1725, Bradford had started the New York Gazette, which published the official opinions of the governor and the Court party. Morris and his partners had Zenger print the New York Weekly Journal.

Governor Cosby was extremely angry about articles published in the Weekly Journal that made fun of him. Although Morris, Alexander, and Smith were the writers and editors of the Weekly Journal, Governor Cosby had John Peter Zenger arrested and tried for treason. Alexander and Smith were both lawyers and planned to defend Zenger, but the leaders of the Court party were able to get them suspended from the trial. The best lawyer in the colonies at the time was thought to be Andrew Hamilton, and he was hired to defend Zenger.

Although many in New York assumed that Zenger would be found guilty for the articles he had printed, Hamilton was able to convince the jury that the case was not just about Zenger. He told them that the issue was liberty versus tyranny. He argued that the press had the right and the responsibility to inform the people of what was going on in the government. Hamilton was very convincing, and the jury only deliberated for a few minutes before they returned to the courtroom. Zenger was declared not guilty.

Many historians see the trial of John Peter Zenger as an important step in defining the rights of colonists when confronted with the tyranny of Crown officials. Others have gone as far as stating that the Zenger case was influential when the Bill of Rights was drawn up and freedom of the press was guaranteed in the First Amendment to the U.S. Constitution. It also showed that people such as Morris, Alexander, and Smith, who were members of the colonial elite, felt they had the right to stand up to the king's royal governor.

ALBANY CONGRESS

In June and July of 1754, representatives from New York, New Hampshire, Massachusetts, Rhode Island, Connecticut, Pennsylva-

Albany Plan

The Albany Plan called for the colonial defenses to be put under the control of one chief military executive and for there to be one commissioner for Indian affairs for all the colonies. In addition, the plan had provisions for a grand council of delegates that would have representatives from all thirteen colonies. The Albany Plan was taken back to the seven colonies that had sent representatives. Not one colonial legislature agreed to the plan. In 1754, there was too much competition between the colonies for them to unite in their common defense. Over the next 20 years, the situation would change drastically.

nia, and Maryland, along with representatives from the League of the Iroquois, met in Albany, New York. This meeting is known as the Albany Congress, and many topics were on the agenda. High on the list were the relations between the colonies and the Iroquois, who had remained allies of the English colonies against the French.

The Iroquois rightly claimed that they were losing land to a number of colonies, that too much rum was being given to their people, and that the fur traders in Albany were still trading with the French and their Native American allies. All these grievances were true, but the colonial representatives denied that there were any problems, and so nothing was accomplished with the Iroquois.

The delegates did agree to work together to try and stop French expansion into the Ohio River Valley. They also agreed to appoint one person to deal with Native Americans for all the colonies. At the Congress, Benjamin Franklin of Pennsylvania and Governor William Shirley of Massachusetts proposed that the colonies form into one union. This was known as the Albany Plan. It was not adopted.

The French and Indian Wars

Starting in 1689 and ending in 1762, France and England fought four different wars in Europe and around the world. In the colonies of North America, the French in Canada allied with numerous Native American tribes fought against the English and their Iroquois allies for the lands between New France and the English colonies of North America. During the almost 75 years from the beginning to the end of the French and Indian wars, the security of the English colonies was a major concern. Often the Crown selected its colonial governors based on military ability rather than the ability to govern.

During the wars, many colonists gained military experience. They also learned a style of fighting that was more like that of the Native Americans than the formal fighting style of Europe at the time. When the American Revolution started shortly after the last of the French and Indian wars, the colonists were able to use their experience against the British troops. The first of these wars was known in Europe as the War of the League of Augsburg. In the English colonies, it was simply called King William's War and was fought from 1689 to 1697.

KING WILLIAM'S WAR
1689–1697

In summer 1689, England declared war on France in Europe. In the French and English colonies of North America, sporadic raids by both sides had already taken place. In the years preceding King William's War, the Iroquois had kept the French isolated in the north. With war in Europe, the fighting in North America became more frequent. Although there was fighting in Maine, New Hampshire, and what is now Nova Scotia, Canada, New York had as much if not more fighting than the other areas.

In February 1690, Governor Frontenac of New France planned to attack the English colonies in three different areas. Maine, New Hampshire, and Albany, New York, were the intended targets. In hopes of neutralizing the Iroquois, he offered to hold peace talks with them. However, this was just a trick to keep the Iroquois from stopping a French and Native American force from sneaking into New York and attacking Albany.

Fearing attack, Albany had sought reinforcements. At the time, Leisler had taken control of New York City, and the people in Albany did not want to recognize his authority. Instead, they asked the colony of Connecticut for help. Connecticut responded by sending almost 100 men to Albany for the winter of 1689–90. Twenty-five of the Connecticut militiamen were sent on to Schenectady, which is 15 miles northwest of Albany.

At Schenectady, approximately 150 Dutch traders and farmers lived with their families and a few African-American slaves. The town was surrounded by a wooden palisade. A force of more than 200 French Canadians and Christianized Native Americans slipped down from Montreal across the ice on Lake Champlain and Lake George. On the night of February 8, 1690, the French force arrived outside the gates of Schenectady.

No official record of the event explains the fact, but when the French force arrived, the only guards at the gate to Schenectady were two snowmen. The French and Native Americans were able to slip into the town undetected. Just before midnight, they started shooting. In short order, approximately 60 residents were killed. A few people were able to escape, and some of the older men and women were left alone. Twenty-seven people were taken captive. The entire town was then set on fire. Sixty-three houses and the Dutch Reformed church were burned down.

Men from Albany and a number of Mohawk warriors pursued the raiding party but were unable to catch them. They did fight one skirmish just before the French and their allies were able to cross the St. Lawrence River back to Montreal. At this

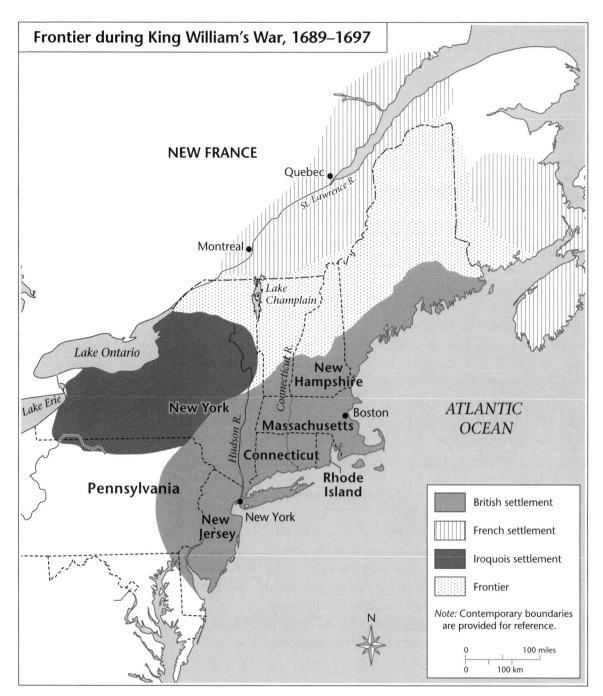

Frontier during King William's War, 1689–1697

NEW FRANCE

Quebec

St. Lawrence R.

Montreal

Lake Champlain

Lake Ontario

Lake Erie

New Hampshire

New York

Connecticut R.

Hudson R.

Massachusetts

Boston

Connecticut

Pennsylvania

Rhode Island

New Jersey

New York

ATLANTIC OCEAN

	British settlement
	French settlement
	Iroquois settlement
	Frontier

Note: Contemporary boundaries are provided for reference.

0   100 miles

0   100 km

N

A large area between the English colonies and New France was the scene of most of the fighting during King William's War and the other wars between the French and the English in North America.

point, the people of Albany were forced to ask Lieutenant Governor Leisler for help. The Connecticut troops went home, and Leisler's future son-in-law Jacob Milborne was sent to help defend Albany. It was at this time that Leisler called a meeting of the English colonies hoping to persuade them to present a united front against the French.

However, the plans for cooperation never really came to pass. The leaders in Massachusetts wanted to attack Port Royal in Nova Scotia by water and then go on to attack Quebec City. The small settlements in Maine and New Hampshire had their own frontiers to defend. Pennsylvania and New Jersey were without governors at the time and were also heavily influenced by the Quakers in those colonies, who followed the practice of pacifism.

When the leaders of New York planned to retaliate for the attack on Schenectady, they hoped to attack the very center of French power in Montreal. However, the planned forces from other colonies never showed up, and there was a disagreement between the Connecticut and New York forces as to who was in charge. Leisler, once again, wanted Milborne to command. The Connecticut militia wanted Major Fitz-John Winthrop as the leader. Winthrop was a former British soldier and the son of the governor of Connecticut. Leisler gave in, and Winthrop was put in charge of the operation, with Milborne in charge of coordinating the supplies for the expedition.

The force reached Albany in July and was confronted with an outbreak of smallpox among both the European and Native American residents of the area. Despite losing part of his force, Major Winthrop pressed north with inadequate supplies. Milborne had assured him that the needed supplies would catch up with Winthrop and his force soon.

Winthrop and his troops made it to Lake Champlain, where they waited for the supplies to reach them. When the supplies did not arrive, Winthrop and most of his men were forced to return to Albany. Captain John Schuyler led a small group of volunteers up the lake into New France. Schuyler's force consisted of approximately 57 colonists and 125 Native Americans. On August 23, 1690, they attacked La Prairie, which is directly across the St. Lawrence River from Montreal. The English force killed six people,

This late 18th-century engraving depicts an Iroquois as a savage holding a tomahawk and a club. *(Library of Congress, Prints and Photographs Division [LC-USZ62-1664])*

took a number of captives, and burned some of the houses in the village. They also shot 150 head of cattle. The Native Americans on the side of the English were reluctant to attack the nearby fort, which was signaling Montreal. Captain Schuyler was forced to retreat to New York. His attack on La Prairie was the only revenge that New York was able to take for the attack on Schenectady.

For much of the rest of the war, it fell to the Iroquois Confederacy to keep the French out of New York. The British officials in New York City made many promises of support and gave the Iroquois many gifts but failed to provide the military support needed to defeat the French. Schuyler led another expedition into Canada but was even less successful when his force was overwhelmed by a much larger French and Indian force.

The home territories of the Mohawk and the Oneida, both members of the Iroquois Confederacy, were attacked by the French. Villages were burned and crops destroyed. During the course of the war, as many as 1,300 Iroquois died in battles and from disease. The colonists in New York, in comparison, only lost about 200 people. However, more than 400 people, or about one quarter of the population in the Albany area, left during the war. When the Treaty of Ryswick was signed in Europe on September 30, 1697, ending the war, the map in North America had changed little. The main outcome of King William's War was the belief on both sides that North America was probably not big enough for both French and English colonies. As long as the two European superpowers vied for control and influence around the world, there would be fighting in North America. In fact, peace lasted for only a few years before Queen Anne's War started in 1702, where the last war had finished off.

QUEEN ANNE'S WAR
1702–1713

After King William's War, the French in North America moved to encircle the English colonies in North America. They pushed westward and established Fort Pontchartrain near modern-day Detroit, Michigan. In the south, the French planned to establish a settlement at the mouth of the Mississippi River. However, they chose a site on Mobile Bay in what is now Alabama. In addition to this, French missionaries were becoming established down along the Mississippi River.

In 1702, there was a controversy in Europe over who would become the next king of Spain. Louis XIV of France's grandson, Phillip, became the king of Spain. Then Louis XIV declared Phillip the heir to the French throne as well. The thought of France and Spain being united under one king was more than Britain and the rest of Europe could accept. On May 4, 1702, the War of the Spanish Succession began.

In North America, it was called Queen Anne's War, after the ruler of Britain at the time. When war broke out again in the Americas, the Iroquois decided this time they would stay out of it. There was fighting throughout New England, in the Carolinas, Spanish Florida, and the Caribbean. The French in Canada wanted to make sure the Iroquois stayed out of this war, and therefore never attacked New York. They would have had to pass through Iroquois territory to get to New York, and it was not worth bringing the Iroquois into the war.

There were people in New York who were willing to get involved in the war. In summer 1709, a large force of colonial mili-

Anne I ruled Great Britain and Ireland from 1702 until 1714. This engraving is from a statue of the leader at Blenheim Palace in Woodstock, England. *(Library of Congress, Prints and Photographs Division [LC-USZ62-110255])*

tia assembled at Albany, New York. The plan was to attack Montreal from the south while a British force attacked up along the St. Lawrence River. During the summer, 1,500 men from New York, Massachusetts, Connecticut, New Jersey, and Pennsylvania made a road through the woods from Albany to Lake Champlain and established two forts along the route. The force waited through the summer and into the fall for the promised British forces. They never arrived, and the expedition against Montreal had to be abandoned.

The war in the colonies faded away long before the Treaty of Utrecht was signed on April 11, 1713. The treaty had only limited impact in the colonies. Its main objective was to try and maintain a balance of power between France and Britain in North America. It was a balance that lasted for a little over 30 years before war once again broke out in Europe and in North America.

KING GEORGE'S WAR
1744–1748

After Queen Anne's War, the people in New York tried to maintain and expand their hold on the lands between themselves and French Canada. In 1728, New York governor William Burnet ordered a trading post be built on Lake Ontario in the hope that some of the fur trade headed down the lake to Montreal could be diverted to New York. The trading post was built near modern-day Oswego. In 1731, the French countered with a move south and built a fort at Crown Point on Lake Champlain. Despite these attempts to move in on each other's territories, no sustained fighting took place until war was once again declared in Europe.

In March 1744, France and Britain once again declared war on each other. This time, the war was called the War of Austrian Succession in Europe and King George's War in North America. The French in North America got word of the outbreak of war first, and a force from Louisbourg on Cape Breton attacked and destroyed the English fishing village of Canseau. In retaliation, a large force from New England with help from New York and other colonies attacked and captured the fort at Louisbourg. The attack was supported by three British naval ships from the Caribbean squadron. The ships were commanded by Commodore Warren, who had lived in New York.

Sir Peter Warren
(1703–1752)

Peter Warren was born in Ireland and entered the British navy at the age of 13. Two of his relatives were admirals in the navy. Warren rose quickly through the ranks, becoming a captain in 1727. In the 1730s, he was assigned to patrol the coast of the English colonies in North America. In 1731, he married Susannah DeLancey, whose brother was chief justice and lieutenant governor of New York. Warren became wealthy from the prize money he received from successfully capturing enemy ships, and he invested in land in New York. At one time, he owned the area of Manhattan that is now Greenwich Village.

Warren was also involved in the fur trade with the Iroquois. He purchased 14,000 acres along the Mohawk River and brought his nephew, William Johnson, over from Ireland to manage his land. Johnson became a friend of the Iroquois and was instrumental in getting them to fight with the English in the French and Indian War (1755–62).

Warren eventually moved to England, where he was made a member of Parliament. On a trip to the family estates in Ireland in 1752, he caught an infection and died within four days. He was buried in Ireland.

Although there had been numerous raids in New England, New York was slow to take direct action in King George's War. The state assembly had been reluctant to pay for military support, and the small force at Saratoga, New York, left because the colony would not pay to improve living conditions at the fort. In November 1745, a force of 300 French and 200 Native Americans came south and attacked the Dutch settlement at Saratoga. Thirty people were killed, and almost 100 people, many of them African-American slaves, were taken prisoner. Most of the houses in the town were burned.

After the attack on Saratoga, the assembly voted to rebuild and garrison the fort there. The French and their allies did not make any other large-scale attacks on New York for a while. Instead they turned to small ambushes. In May 1746, a dozen men were killed in an ambush between Albany and Schenectady.

Early in 1747, the Iroquois were finally convinced to enter into the war on the side of the English colonies. Three thousand troops assembled at Albany with the plan of attacking the French fort at Crown Point. However, there were a number of problems. The militia from New York and Pennsylvania mutinied because they had not been paid. Governor Clinton of New York was waiting for money from London to pay the troops, and it arrived too late for the attack on Crown Point. When Clinton finally got the money in July, he paid the troops and then let them go home. The Iroquois felt betrayed. They had entered the war to help the English colonists who then did not fight.

On June 30, 1747, the French once again attacked Saratoga. This time, there was a large force at the new fort that repelled the French. The commander of the fort thought the French force was quite small. He sent Lieutenant Joseph Chew with a force of about 100 to pursue the French. It turned out that they were chasing between 500 and 600 French and Native Americans. Fifteen of Chew's troops were killed and around 50 captured. A relief force from Albany was able to hang on to the fort for a short time before they retreated and the fort was burned.

The war ended in 1748 with no real winner in North America. Much to the disappointment of people in the colonies, England gave Louisbourg back to the French in exchange for Madras, a French-held outpost in India. It would take one more war to settle the issue finally of who would control North America.

FRENCH AND INDIAN WAR
(Seven Years' War)
1755–1762

The first three wars in North America between the French and English colonies were extensions of wars in Europe. When war was declared again in 1755, it was because of the conflict in North America. Both the French in Canada and the English colonists, especially those in Virginia, looked to all the lands between the Appalachian Mountains and the Mississippi River, and particularly the Ohio River Valley, as a necessary prize for colonial expansion and profit.

In the early years of the French and Indian War, the French and their Native American allies held the upper hand. They built forts throughout the Ohio River Valley and strengthened their hold

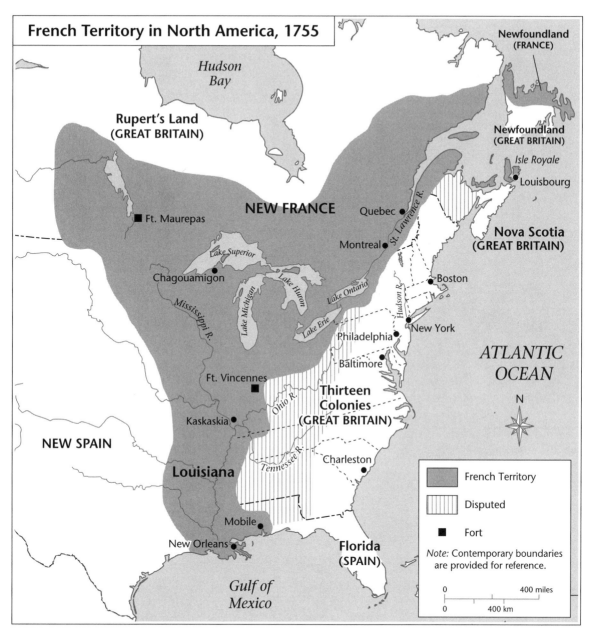

French Territory in North America, 1755

Hudson Bay

Rupert's Land
(GREAT BRITAIN)

Newfoundland
(FRANCE)

Newfoundland
(GREAT BRITAIN)

Isle Royale

Louisbourg

NEW FRANCE

Ft. Maurepas

Quebec

St. Lawrence R.

Montreal

Nova Scotia
(GREAT BRITAIN)

Lake Superior

Chagouamigon

Lake Michigan

Lake Huron

Lake Ontario

Boston

Mississippi R.

Lake Erie

Hudson R.

New York

Philadelphia

Ft. Vincennes

Ohio R.

Baltimore

NEW SPAIN

Kaskaskia

Thirteen
Colonies
(GREAT BRITAIN)

ATLANTIC
OCEAN

N

Louisiana

Tennessee R.

Charleston

French Territory

Disputed

Fort

Mobile

New Orleans

Florida
(SPAIN)

Note: Contemporary boundaries
are provided for reference.

0   400 miles

0   400 km

Gulf of
Mexico

By 1755, the French had expanded their territory into the Ohio River Valley and down the Mississippi River to encircle the English colonies.

along the St. Lawrence River and the Great Lakes. The English plan was to attack the French in three different regions. The forts in the west were one objective. Louisbourg and the mouth of the St.

During a battle at Fort William Henry, the marquis de Montcalm, commander of the French forces during the French and Indian War, led an attack against the British at Fort William Henry and then attempted to prevent the Native Americans from killing many of the captured British. *(Library of Congress, Prints and Photographs Division [LC-USZ62-120704])*

Lawrence River were another. The final thrust would be in New York as the British planned to drive the French back to the north and cut off their access to the west.

At first, the colonials and their British support performed poorly. In 1755, at Lake George, New York, a large force of colonial soldiers intended to take Crown Point. Another force was sent to take Fort Niagara. William Johnson was in charge of the attack on Crown Point and began by building two forts at the head of Lake George—Fort George and Fort William Henry. The French left Crown Point on September 1, 1755, with 3,200 French and Native Americans to catch the primarily colonial force at Fort Edwards on the Hudson River.

Along the way, the French commander, Baron Dieskau, learned that Johnson was at Lake George and had not finished his fortifications there. The French decided to change their plan. Johnson sent out 1,000 troops to meet the French not knowing that their force was more than 3,200 French and Native American fighters. In what turned out to be one of the bloodiest battles of the war, the colonials were mowed down by the French and forced to retreat. When the French rushed to catch them, they ran into Johnson's main force, which was dug in and had artillery support. This time, the French were forced to withdraw. It looked like the day would end in a draw, but as the French retreated, they ran into a relief column coming from Fort Edwards. Many of the French and most of their supplies were captured.

Although the colonials had won the day, they were forced to abandon their objective of capturing Crown Point. Governor Shirley of Massachusetts led the attack on Niagara and fared even

Sir William Johnson
(1715–1774)

William Johnson was the Irish-born nephew of Sir Peter Warren, who came to New York in 1738 to manage his uncle's 14,000-acre tract along the Mohawk River. He used his location to enter into trade with the Iroquois and became a respected and close friend of many of the Mohawk who lived in his area. In 1746, Johnson was appointed by Governor George Clinton to be superintendent of Iroquois affairs for the colony.

Thanks to Johnson, the Iroquois joined the British in the French and Indian War. In addition to his victory at Lake George, he was instrumental in the eventual capture of Fort Niagara in 1759 and took part in the capture of Montreal in 1760. In 1762, he founded Johnstown, New York, northwest of Albany. Johnson was well respected among the Iroquois and was in part responsible for keeping many of them loyal to the British. One of the reasons for his influence among the Iroquois and especially the Mohawk was his relationship with Molly Brant. Molly Brant was the sister of the Mohawk leader Joseph Brant and was considered by many to be Johnson's wife. Together Johnson and Molly Brant had a number of children. Although Johnson's older English children by his first wife inherited his estates, Molly Brant was well provided for and remained an influential member of the Iroquois community for many years.

Fort George and Fort William Henry were located at the south end of Lake George, pictured in this mid-19th-century Currier & Ives lithograph. *(Library of Congress, Prints and Photographs Division [LC-USZ62-30513])*

worse. His supplies never fully reached him at Oswego, and so no attempt was made on Fort Niagara. It would take a long time before the British committed the resources that were needed to finally defeat the French in North America.

Before the tide turned against the French, they built Fort Ticonderoga further south on Lake Champlain. The first attempt by the British to take the fort in the summer of 1758 ended in a sound defeat. It looked like the French would be able to hold on to Canada indefinitely. However, William Pitt came to power in England and was determined to win at any cost. He turned the full force of his government to winning the war in North America. To do so, he was forced to amass a huge debt. It was the attempt to get the American colonies to pay their share of the debt that would be in part responsible for the American Revolution.

On July 26, 1758, the fort at Louisbourg finally fell to the English and the end of the war was near. The English navy made it almost impossible for the French to send supplies to their forces in Canada. And it was just a matter of time before the original objective of the war was achieved. On July 25, 1759, a combined force of British regulars under General Prideaux and colonial militia led by William Johnson captured Fort Niagara. At the other side of New York, on the next day, Fort Ticonderoga fell to the British.

By fall 1759, the British had captured Quebec City and all that remained of New France was Montreal. In 1760, Montreal fell. Although it took more than two years for the terms of the Treaty of Paris to be worked out, England now controlled all of North America east of the Mississippi River, except New Orleans. Now it was time to pay for the war.

8

The Road to Revolution

The end of the French and Indian War in 1762 brought many changes to the British colonies of North America. Peace did not bring prosperity to New York and many of the other colonies. Many colonial merchants and farmers had made large profits supplying the war effort. With the large military contracts gone, there was an overall economic recession in New York, especially in New York City. At the same time, Parliament in London decided that the American colonies should shoulder their share of the £127 million debt that Britain had built up during the war.

By the 1760s, many of the people in the colonies had lost the feeling of connection that the early settlers had had with England. The majority of people in North America were now native born. Many of the new immigrants were coming from other countries in Europe and never felt any loyalty to the English king. To complicate the situation, it had become the accepted political belief that government was based on elected representation. Parliament had no representatives from the colonies, and therefore many felt it should not have the authority to tax the colonies. In the time between the end of the French and Indian War and the Declaration of Independence in 1776, this difference between the patriots in the colonies and the government in London was the central point in the growing rebellion.

THE SUGAR ACT
April 5, 1764

The first attempt by the Crown to get the colonies to help pay down the war debt was known as the Sugar Act of 1764. The Sugar Act was intended to reform the Molasses Act of 1733 that had tried to limit the importation of molasses and sugar from non-British sources. The Molasses Act had not worked primarily because it was ignored by the colonial merchants. They either did not pay the customs duties or smuggled in untaxed molasses.

The Sugar Act reduced the tax substantially and set up a better way for the taxes to be collected. In the past, customs officers were forced to bring their cases before local courts, and this made it almost impossible to convict smugglers and tax evaders. New rules were created that allowed customs cases to be heard in special Admiralty Courts away from the influence of local juries.

Most people in the colonies were unaffected by the Sugar Act. The merchants it did affect most likely figured they could avoid this tax just as they had earlier ones. The major problem with the Sugar Act from the standpoint of the Crown was it failed to generate enough revenue. A new tax would have to be devised if the colonies were going to pay up.

THE STAMP ACT
March 22, 1765

The solution to the problem for London was the Stamp Act. This was not something new. In fact, the colonial assembly in New York had already used a stamp system to raise tax revenues for the colony. Various stamp taxes were also in place in Britain. The Stamp Act of 1765 was going to require that a stamp be purchased and affixed to any legal documents, printed materials, and consumer goods such as playing cards. The Stamp Act

When affixed to goods, this stamp signified that a tax must be paid upon purchase. Many colonists felt that the British unfairly introduced these taxes when they implemented the Stamp Act in 1765, which affected goods ranging from business transactions to playing cards. *(Library of Congress, Prints and Photographs Division [LC-USZ61-539])*

set off a series of protests in the colonies that had never been seen before. The idea of taxation without representation upset many people in the colonies.

In New York, reaction to the Stamp Act was swift and at times violent. The Stamp Act, passed in March 1765, was to go into effect on November 1, 1765. During the time in between, the sleeping giant of American patriotism was awakened. Throughout the colonies, groups calling themselves the Sons of Liberty were formed to take a leadership role in organizing protests against the Stamp Act.

New York was one of the most active colonies in organizing protests against the Stamp Act. The colonial political leaders were quick to answer Massachusetts's call for a colonial congress to discuss a cooperative effort to stop the Stamp Act. The Stamp Act Congress was held in New York City from October 7 to 25, 1765. The representatives from the nine colonies who sent delegates agreed to appeal directly to England with a petition to the king. The petition opened with a statement of loyalty from the delegates. Very few people at this point were thinking of independence for the colonies; they just wanted to protest the idea of the tax. They wrote, "that it is inseparably essential to the Freedom of a People, and the undoubted right of Englishmen, that no taxes be imposed on them, but with their own Consent, given personally, or by their Representatives."

The petition for the most part was ignored. However, on the day that the act was scheduled to take place, no Crown official in the colonies dared issue the stamps. In New York City, on November 1, 1765, two mobs formed at either end of the town and soon joined in front of the walls of Fort George. The combined group numbered more than 2,000 people. Each group carried an effigy, or figure, of Lieutenant Governor Cadwallader Colden.

One group had broken into Colden's carriage house and stolen a carriage and a sleigh. The other group had built a portable gallows. When they reached the fort, they hurled insults and bricks at the soldiers inside. They then hanged one effigy and burned the other along with the carriage and sleigh. Major Thomas James, the commander of the fort, had been quoted as saying he would ram the Stamp Act down the throats of New Yorkers with his sword. Knowing this, the mob went on to his mansion and ransacked it. They also carried off all the major's wine.

Many colonists in New York actively protested the Stamp Act. Here colonists parade to express their displeasure. *(Library of Congress, Prints and Photographs Division [LC-USZ61-536])*

In addition to the protests in the streets, a general boycott of British imports was organized. Farmers were urged to plant more flax and raise more sheep so the colonists could produce their own

The Sons of Liberty

Throughout the colonies, the most radical patriots formed into groups to protest the Stamp Act. One of the opponents of the Stamp Act in the British House of Commons, Isaac Barré, called the protestors the "sons of liberty." Soon the name spread to the colonies where it was readily adopted. In New York City, the leaders of the Sons of Liberty were Alexander McDougal, John Lamb, and Isaac Sears.

The Sons of Liberty held regular demonstrations in the streets of New York City. They also held outdoor meetings at spots designated by a liberty pole or a liberty tree. The leaders of the group wrote articles for the newspapers and had pamphlets printed, which urged the people to act. The Sons of Liberty were often at the forefront of the protests that eventually led to the War for Independence.

Protesting English rule, the Sons of Liberty pull down a statue of George III, located near the Bowling Green, in July 1776. *(Library of Congress, Prints and Photographs Division [LC-USZ62-2455])*

Colonists denounce the Stamp Act in 1765. *(Library of Congress)*

linen and woolen materials. Many people also stopped drinking tea. Tea and cloth were major imports. The efforts of the patriots were effective. The Stamp Act was repealed in March 1766 without a stamp ever being issued. When the Stamp Act was repealed, Parliament passed the Declaratory Act later in 1766, which stated that they still reserved the right to make laws for the colonies. This is something they would do repeatedly, which would cause a continuing decline in relations between London and the American colonies.

THE TOWNSHEND DUTIES
June 29, 1767

Parliament's next attempt at taxing the colonies came in June 1767, when it passed a series of taxes on goods imported into the colonies. This type of tax is known as a duty and was proposed by Charles Townshend, one of the leaders of the government in London. A tax cut for people in Britain forced Parliament to once again propose taxing the colonies. In addition, the government had recently learned that the New York assembly had refused to support the British troops in the colony as required under the Quartering Act of 1765. New York had become the North American headquarters for the British military and was expected to provide support for the regular soldiers stationed in the colony.

Members of Parliament agreed with some of the colonial leaders who asserted that part of the problem with the Stamp Act was the fact that it was a direct internal tax on the colonies. Townshend Duties were seen as an external tax the colonists would not object to. Duties were to be paid on glass, lead, painter's colors, paper, and tea. The money from the duties was intended to pay Crown officials in the colonies, freeing them from any obligation to local government. The law also further strengthened the Admiralty Courts and the system of customs collections.

The protest of the Townshend Duties was not as overwhelming as the reaction to the Stamp Act. However, friction between the colonials and the Crown and its customs officials continued to grow. Boston was one of the hotbeds of the dissent over the Town-

Battle of Golden Hill
(January 18, 1770)

As part of the conflict between British soldiers and Patriots in New York City, the soldiers had regularly cut down liberty poles that had been erected by the Patriots to identify meeting places. On January 16, 1770, New York Patriots issued broadsides (posters) complaining about the soldiers and suggesting that New York employers should refrain from hiring them. The soldiers, or "redcoats" as they were called by the colonials, retaliated with their own broadsides giving their side of the situation. A couple of the soldiers distributing the broadsides were beaten by local workers.

On January 18, 1770, a large group of soldiers cut down the liberty pole on Golden Hill and a riot broke out. Blood was drawn on both sides with the soldiers using their bayonets on some of the colonials. This was the first violent clash between American Patriots and British soldiers. Six weeks later, the Battle of Golden Hill was followed by the Boston Massacre where a similar crowd of Patriots confronted a group of British soldiers. Only in Boston they did not wait for the mob to get close enough to use their bayonets. The soldiers fired into the crowd and killed five people.

shend Duties, and riots took place in June 1768, when customs officials seized a ship that belonged to John Hancock. In New York, bad feelings grew between the British troops and workers in the city. Soldiers were allowed to hire themselves out as laborers when they were off-duty. The city had not yet recovered financially, and many civilian workers found it hard to find work. This led to a confrontation between the workers and soldiers.

The Townshend Duties had failed to raise the expected revenue. So, after the conflicts in New York and Boston, Parliament decided to repeal all the duties except the one on tea. The duty on tea was kept to show the colonials that Parliament still believed they had the right to tax them. With the Townshend Duties all but gone, the troubles in the colonies decreased. In New York, as well as many of the other colonies, the economy was improving after the postwar recession, and people were feeling good about their situation. If the king and Parliament had wanted to, they could have resolved their remaining differences with the Americans and hung on to the colonies. However, King George III considered the colonies misbehaving children and was more interested in further punishing them than he was in giving them additional rights.

THE TEA ACT
May 10, 1773

After three years of relative calm in the American colonies, Britain gave the Patriots reason to renew their protests. On May 10, 1773, Parliament passed the Tea Act. The act was intended to help the struggling British East India Company avoid bankruptcy by giving it a tea monopoly in the American colonies. Before the Tea Act, British tea was shipped from its Asian colonies to Britain and taxed there. Then it was repackaged and shipped to American colonies where it was taxed again under the remaining Townshend Duty. This made the tea very expensive, and most people in the colonies drank Dutch tea that was smuggled into the colonies.

Under the Tea Act, the British East India Company was allowed to ship tea directly to the North American colonies. This made British tea cheaper in the colonies while at the same time increasing revenues under the Townshend Duty. The Patriots in the colonies saw this as another attempt by Parliament to regulate the colonies without their consent. When the first load of tea arrived

New York Tea Party

Although the Boston Tea Party is the most famous, it was by no means the only tea party. A number of colonies had their own versions of a "tea party." In New York, the Sons of Liberty had to wait until April 22, 1774, for a shipment of tea to be brought in. The governor of New York, William Tryon, made an agreement with the British tea agent in New York that any ships carrying tea would be sent back to England. The captain of the ship *London* lied about his cargo and tried to sneak a shipment of British tea into New York. When the Sons of Liberty heard rumors that the tea had arrived, they followed Boston's example. A number of people disguised as "Mohawk" boarded the *London* and dumped 18 chests of tea into the harbor.

George III ruled Great Britain and Ireland from 1760 until 1820. *(Library of Congress, Prints and Photographs Division [LC-USZ62-7819])*

in Boston Harbor on December 16, 1773, approximately 60 members of Boston's Sons of Liberty disguised as Native Americans boarded three ships in Boston and threw £10,000 worth of tea into Boston Harbor.

When the tea was dumped into Boston harbor, King George III and the government in London decided it was time to teach the upstart Patriots in the colony a lesson. They passed a series of laws that finally brought about the American rebellion.

THE INTOLERABLE ACTS 1774

Parliament called them the Coercive Acts, and they were intended to force the colonists to recognize the authority of the government in London. In the colonies, they were simply called the Intolerable Acts. Although none of the acts had a direct effect on the people of New York, everyone in the colonies saw that the king and Parliament believed they had complete and arbitrary control over the colonies.

The first part of the acts was called the Boston Port Bill. It closed Boston Harbor until such time as the tea that had been dumped in the harbor was paid for. The second part was the Massachusetts Government Act, which changed Massachusetts's charter, taking power away from the people of the colony and giving it to Crown officials. The Administration of Justice Act made it legal for British officials to move trials for crimes against royal laws anywhere in the empire. This was enacted to prevent local juries from being lenient with their neighbors and friends. The final part of the acts was the Quebec Act. This gave the people of Canada special rights. They were allowed to remain Catholics and continue to own lands under the system set up by the French. Canada was also given all the land between the Appalachian Mountains and the Mississippi River. Many colonials had fought in the French and Indian War so those lands would be available for colonial expansion.

The major impact of the Intolerable Acts was that people for the first time saw the Crown interfering directly with rights that Americans had come to assume were inviolate. Throughout the colonies, people relied on the Committees of Correspondence to communicate ways to deal with the Intolerable Acts. With the harbor closed in Boston, the people of Massachusetts were cut off from receiving many needed goods. In New York, and elsewhere,

Committees of Correspondence

In the 18th century, it was difficult to communicate ideas and information over long distances. There were very few newspapers in the colonies, and none of the electronic media that people depend on today existed. The Boston, Massachusetts, town meeting decided in 1772 to set up a committee that would "state the Rights of the Colonists" and share them with other communities in Massachusetts. This first Committee of Correspondence worked so well that the idea soon spread to all of the colonies. It was through the Committees of Correspondence that the call for the First Continental Congress went out.

people organized relief efforts. Food and other goods were shipped overland and to other Massachusetts ports to help the people of the Boston area.

It was the New York Committee of Correspondence that first called for a Continental Congress to come up with a unified response to the Intolerable Acts. The idea took hold throughout the colonies, and the First Continental Congress was to be held in Philadelphia in fall 1774.

THE FIRST CONTINENTAL CONGRESS

The idea had come from New York, but 12 of the thirteen colonies sent delegates to Philadelphia to participate in the First Continental Congress. Only Georgia did not send any delegates. The delegates from New York were John Alsop, James Duane, John Jay, Phillip Livingston, and Isaac Low. Many in New York were expecting the Congress to resolve the differences between London and the colonies. But George III had drawn his line in the sand, and the colonials were not going to back down.

John Jay
(1745–1829)

John Jay was one of a handful of men who were instrumental in shaping the struggle between Britain and its American colonies. He was a political conservative who had been born in New York and educated at King's College (now Columbia University). Jay came from one of the wealthy families of New York. His family was one of the few among the New York elite to join the Patriot cause.

Jay wanted to avoid war but was not willing to give in on the principles of the colonies. At the First Continental Congress, he drafted the Congress's response, called the Address to the People of Great Britain.

He helped write New York's first constitution and served as the state's chief justice.

At the Second Continental Congress, he served as the president of the Congress. Along with John Adams and Benjamin Franklin, Jay negotiated the treaty that ended the American Revolution. Under the Articles of Confederation, he served as the secretary of foreign affairs. When the U.S. Constitution was ratified, George Washington appointed him chief justice of the Supreme Court. He later left the court and served two terms as the governor of the state of New York.

The Congress decided to outline their position to the king and then agreed upon three economic steps that they hoped would force King George III to back down. Their first step was to call for a boycott of all British and Irish imports that would start on December 1, 1774. This would be followed on March 1, 1775, by a call for the people of the colonies not to consume British and certain other foreign goods. If the king had still not backed down, the Congress called for an embargo on all American exports to England, Ireland, and the British islands of the Caribbean.

The majority of the delegates at the First Continental Congress expected reconciliation with England and wanted to avoid war. In the Resolutions of the First Continental Congress, the delegates included the following:

John Jay represented New York at the First Continental Congress. *(Library of Congress, Prints and Photographs Division [LC-USZ61-295])*

> To these grievous acts and measures, Americans cannot submit, but in hopes that their fellow subjects in Great-Britain will, on a revision of them, restore us to that state in which both countries found happiness and prosperity, we have for the present only resolved to pursue the following peaceable measures. . . .

Despite the peaceful intentions of the Congress, fighting broke out in Massachusetts in the spring of 1775, and there was no turning back from a war for American independence.

9

War for Independence

On April 19, 1775, the Battles of Lexington and Concord in Massachusetts took the conflict between Britain and its American colonies from a battle of words and boycotts to one of war. Paul Revere, the Boston silversmith who rode out and sounded the alarm that the British were marching to Lexington and Concord, headed for New York to spread the word of the outbreak of fighting. In New York City, hundreds of Patriots took to the streets. They broke into British storehouses and armed themselves. The British troops retreated to the warship *Asia*, and they were soon followed by the royal governor, William Tryon.

The Patriots had easily taken over New York City. Elections were held throughout the colony, and a provincial congress was set up to steer the colony toward independence. The provincial congress selected members to attend the Second Continental Congress. The British forces were centering their efforts on Boston, where they held the city against a growing force of colonial militia and, eventually, George Washington and the Continental army. The siege of Boston lasted until March 1776. It might have lasted longer had not two forts in upstate New York been captured by Patriots.

FORT TICONDEROGA

On May 10, 1775, Ethan Allen and a group of Vermonters known as the "Green Mountain Boys" snuck up on Fort Ticonderoga on Lake Champlain and captured it without firing a shot. Two days

Ethan Allen led the Green Mountain Boys. This painting dramatizes their capture of Fort Ticonderoga. *(Library of Congress, Prints and Photographs Division [LC-USZ62-96539])*

later on May 12, Seth Warner, Allen's cousin, did the same to the fort at Crown Point. Benedict Arnold, who was with them, went north and captured St. John's, Quebec, Canada, on May 16, 1775.

When George Washington took over the siege of Boston, his army lacked the cannons needed to force the British out of Boston. Someone remembered the cannons at Ticonderoga and Crown Point. Henry Knox was sent north during the winter of 1776 to bring the forts' cannons to Boston. The cannons were placed on sleds and dragged more than 250 miles over the snow to Boston. When they were set up on Dorchester Heights on the night of March 4–5, 1776, overlooking the British in Boston and its harbor, the siege of Boston ended. On March 17, 1776, the

Vermont and the Green Mountain Boys

At the time of the Revolution, there was an area of conflicting claims between New York and New Hampshire. The area was thinly populated. In 1764, the king's Privy Council ruled that the area that would eventually become Vermont was part of New York. Many people in the area had received their land claims from New Hampshire. The people of Vermont, under the leadership of Ethan Allen, his two brothers Ira and Levi, and his cousin Seth Warner, organized a militia known as the Green Mountain Boys to prevent New York officials from taking over their land.

When fighting broke out against the British, Ethan Allen and the Green Mountain boys fought as patriots to drive the British out of Ticonderoga and Crown Point. On January 15, 1777, the people of Vermont declared their independence from both New Hampshire and New York. They created an independent republic. Vermont remained independent until it was admitted to the Union as the 14th state on March 4, 1791.

British commander, General William Howe, decided to evacuate Boston and withdrew his forces to Halifax, Nova Scotia.

THE BATTLE FOR NEW YORK

The evacuation of Boston and New York by the British must have given some people a sense of false hope that the American Revolution would be short and relatively painless. Nothing could have been further from the truth. The British were just regrouping while reinforcements came from England. John Adams, the Massachusetts Patriot leader, is reported to have told George Washington that New York was the "key to the whole continent." With the British gone from Boston, Washington moved his army to New York, planning to defend the city and the area from a British invasion.

When the British returned, they came in force. At the end of June 1776, the first part of the British fleet arrived in 127 ships with 10,000 troops and General Howe in charge. On July 3, 1776, 9,300 British soldiers landed on Staten Island. On July 12, General Howe's brother, Admiral Richard Howe, arrived with 150 more ships and 11,000 additional soldiers. The brothers Howe still held back as they waited for another fleet with additional troops coming

Hessians

To ensure they had sufficient troops to fight the American rebels, the British hired German mercenaries called Hessians. These were professional soldiers who were used in a variety of ways by the British.

north from Charleston, South Carolina. By the time all three groups were in New York, General Howe had 32,000 men under his command, which included a large number of Hessian mercenaries.

General Washington and his men were trying to fortify the area. The colonial forces numbered as many as 28,000 men, but only 19,000 of them were fit enough to take the field against the British. While the British waited for all their forces, and the colonials tried to prepare for the battle to come, the Second Continental Congress was busy preparing the Declaration of Independence. On July 4, 1776, the Declaration of Independence was passed by the Congress. On July 9, 1776, George Washington gathered his men together and had the Declaration of Independence read to them.

After hearing the Declaration of Independence, the people of New York City tore down a statue of King George III that had

George Washington helped assemble and led the Continental army during the Revolutionary War. *(Library of Congress)*

New York and the Declaration of Independence

As the Declaration of Independence took shape in Philadelphia, it had been decided that all the colonies had to agree on the final document. When the first poll of the representatives was taken, nine of the delegations were in favor, two were opposed, and one delegation, that of New York, refused to tell how they would vote. South Carolina and Delaware, which had been opposed to the Declaration, changed their votes, and on July 2, 1776, another preliminary vote was taken. The vote was 12-0 with New York still abstaining. While minor changes were made to the final draft of the Declaration, New York's delegates, William Floyd, Francis Lewis, Philip Livingston, and Lewis Morris, let it be known that when the final vote came on July 4, 1776, New York would make it unanimous, and all four delegates signed their names on the final copy.

The First Paragraph of the Declaration of Independence

When in the Course of human events, it becomes necessary for one people to dissolve the political bands which have connected them with another, and to assume among the Powers of the earth, the separate and equal station to which the Laws of Nature and of Nature's God entitle them, a decent respect to the opinions of mankind requires that they should declare the causes which impel them to the separation.

been put up at the Bowling Green. The statue was supposedly melted down and used for bullets. Throughout the summer, the Patriots waited. In August, the battle drew near.

The first part of the struggle to hang on to New York is known as the Battle of Long Island. Washington had fortified a line on the west-

Under the command of General William Howe, the British defeated the colonial forces during the Battle of Long Island. This lithograph illustrates the Patriots' retreat. *(Library of Congress, Prints and Photographs Division [LC-USZC4-3362])*

British prison ships such as the *Jersey* were used to hold captured Patriots.
(Library of Congress, Prints and Photographs Division [LC-USZ62-124949])

ern end of Long Island in hopes of blocking the British entry to Manhattan. General Howe spent four days doing reconnaissance on Washington's position. On August 27, 10,000 Americans faced 20,000 regular British and Hessian soldiers as Howe attacked Washington's unprotected eastern flank. The British worked to surround Washington's army and forced it back to the fortified Brooklyn Heights.

More than 2,000 Americans were killed, wounded, or captured. Many of the captured were imprisoned on ships such as the *Jersey*, which remained anchored in New York harbor. The British losses were only 400 men. Had Howe pushed his advantage on Brooklyn Heights, the Revolution might have ended in that one battle. However, Howe decided to prepare to bombard the Heights. Realizing the futility of his position, Washington took advantage of a foggy summer night to slip back across the East River with all his troops and equipment. It had not been a good day for the Patriot forces, and the situation would get much worse.

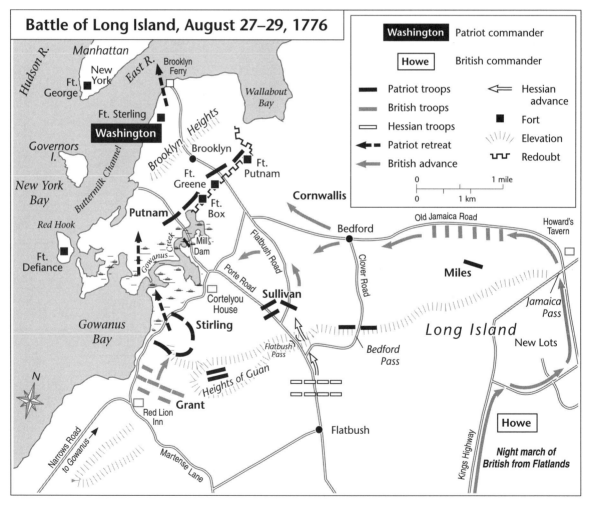

The Battle of Long Island was the first in a series of defeats for the American forces that would leave the British in control of New York until 1783.

After the Battle of Long Island, General Howe waited and tried to negotiate with members of the Continental Congress as private citizens. He refused to recognize the Congress as an official body. When Benjamin Franklin, John Adams, and Edward Rutledge came from the Congress in Philadelphia, Howe told them that before any serious talks could take place, the Congress would have to rescind the Declaration of Independence and pledge their allegiance to Britain. The Patriots knew it was too late for that, and there was no further room for discussion.

On September 15, 1776, General Howe restarted his efforts to capture New York. Washington had planned for the defense of New York City, but many of the militia had deserted after the Battle of Long Island. Nathanael Greene was the Patriot commander at Kip's Bay on Manhattan, when at 11:00 A.M., five British warships sailed into position and opened fire. In the face of the naval broadsides, the militia were quickly routed.

General Howe was able to land 4,000 soldiers without facing any resistance. George Washington had fortified Harlem Heights and had ridden down the island when he heard the ships firing. The American troops were so disorganized that Washington was almost captured as he tried to get the soldiers to stop and fight. The Americans were driven north until there were 10,000 men at Harlem Heights. There were another 18,000 colonial soldiers to the north at Kingsbridge, but of the total force under Washington's command, just over half were fit to fight.

The British now controlled the southern part of Manhattan, and Howe prepared his assault on Harlem Heights. On September 20, 1776, a serious fire started in New York City. Before it burned itself out, 500 buildings were destroyed. The cause of the fire is unknown. However, Washington is reported to have said, "Providence or some good honest fellow had done more for us than we were disposed to do for ourselves."

On September 22, Howe executed Nathan Hale, who had been captured as a spy. Howe planned to outflank the Americans, and on October 12, he sent 4,000 troops to Throg's Neck, where they were going to come back to Manhattan on a causeway. The Americans were able to drive them back. Although the defense of Harlem Heights was seen as a victory for the colonial forces, Washington and his aides decided they did not have the resources to hold off the British for very long.

Nathan Hale
(1755–1776)

Nathan Hale was from Connecticut and had risen to the rank of captain based on his performance during the siege of Boston and the Battle of Long Island. In September 1776, he volunteered to try and spy on the British in Lower Manhattan. He posed as an unemployed Dutch school teacher and was able to gather a lot of information about the British troops before he was captured. Before he was hanged on September 22, 1776, he is reported to have said, "I only regret that I have but one life to lose for my country."

This statue honors Nathan Hale, a spy captured and hanged by the British during the Revolutionary War. *(Library of Congress, Prints and Photographs Division [LC-USZ6-195])*

On October 18, the Americans retreated, leaving all of Manhattan, except Fort Washington, to the British. Over the next month, Howe moved slowly from New Rochelle to Mamaroneck to White Plains, where he once again engaged the Americans. The power and precision of the professional British and Hessian forces were more than the barely trained and undisciplined Americans could handle. After White Plains, Washington lost many of his militia units as their term of service expired, and many others just left.

On November 16, 1776, Fort Washington, which had been hastily built on Harlem Heights to try and prevent the British from sailing up the Hudson River, was attacked by the British. Three thousand patriots had been left to defend the fort, and all those who were not killed in the battle were captured along with their supplies and equipment. Hearing that Fort Washington had fallen, a similar fort on the New Jersey side of the river, Fort Lee, was abandoned before it too was captured.

Washington and his entire army now retreated across New Jersey with the British in hot pursuit. The Americans reached the Delaware River and crossed into Pennsylvania just in time. Had Howe been able to cross the Delaware River, the Revolution would

Margaret Corbin
(1751–1800)

During the Revolution, a number of women became involved in the fighting on the Patriot side. One of these women was Margaret Corbin. In 1772, Margaret married John Corbin, who joined the Pennsylvania Artillery when the Revolution began. The Pennsylvania Artillery was positioned inside Fort Washington when the British attacked on November 16, 1776. Margaret had followed her husband as he served in the military, and she was at Fort Washington when he was killed during a charge by Hessian mercenaries. Margaret Corbin had been helping her husband load a cannon during the battle. When her husband fell, she continued to fire his cannon at the advancing British. Before the end of the battle, she was shot in the chest and nearly lost an arm. Little is known of what happened to Margaret Corbin after the battle. It is known that she was living near West Point, New York, when she died in 1800.

have ended in 1776. However, Washington made sure there were no boats left on the New Jersey side of the river for the British to use. Howe returned to New York for the winter. The British were firmly in control of the southern tier of New York and would continue to hold it until 1783.

THE BATTLE FOR THE REST OF NEW YORK

General Howe apparently considered New York as important as John Adams and other American leaders did. After driving the Patriots out of Manhattan and the lower regions of the state, he turned his attention to the north. If the British captured Albany and created an unbroken British territory from Canada down the Hudson River to New York City, they would be able to cut off New England and its large population from supporting the war in the Midatlantic and southern states.

To accomplish this, Howe devised a three-pronged attack. His own forces would come up the Hudson River and attack Albany from the south. General Burgoyne would bring his army of 9,000 men down from Canada. The third prong was to come from Fort Oswego on Lake Ontario. Colonel Barry Saint Leger led this force that was about 1,200 strong and consisted of Hessians, British regulars, Iroquois, and American Loyalists.

In late summer, the plan was put into motion, but Howe had changed his mind. Instead of heading north to Albany, he took his forces by water to the head of Chesapeake Bay. From there, he attacked and captured Philadelphia. Saint Leger's force stopped on their way to Albany to try and capture Fort Stanwix near Oriskany, New York. Five hundred Patriots manned the fort and were vastly outnumbered by the combined British force. However, they refused to surrender.

On August 6, 1777, American brigadier general Nicholas Herkimer arrived to relieve the fort with 800 New York militia. The battle between his forces and Saint Leger's that took place near Oriskany has been called the bloodiest of the Revolution. For six hours, the two forces used rifles, bayonets, and tomahawks in vicious fighting. When the British finally retreated at the end of the day, each side had lost approximately 200 men, and numerous others were wounded. Saint Leger was forced to return to Oswego, and Burgoyne was left on his own.

The Iroquois and the Revolution

When fighting broke out between the British and their American colonies, both sides tried to get the Iroquois to fight with them. The Iroquois still controlled almost all of western New York and much of the Ohio River Valley. The part of the Intolerable Acts that placed control of the lands between the Appalachian Mountains and the Mississippi River in the hands of the British in Canada was seen by the Iroquois as their only hope of keeping the colonials out of their lands.

Although a few Iroquois fought on the side of the Patriots, most of those who entered into the conflict fought on the side of the British. During the war, many of the Iroquois villages were destroyed by Americans. At the end of the war, many Iroquois relocated to Canada, where they thought it would be safer to live. One of the Iroquois leaders of the time was the Mohawk Joseph Brant (Thayendanegea). He had grown up close to the estate of Sir William Johnson and had fought with Johnson during the French and Indian War. Brant attended a school for Native Americans in Lebanon, Connecticut, where he was converted to Christianity and was taught to speak English and dress like an Englishman. Brant's sister Molly married Johnson. During the Revolution, Brant fought with the British. After the war, he led a group of Mohawk to settle in Ontario, Canada. Several places in Ontario—Brant's Town, Brantford, and Brant County—are named after him.

Joseph Brant (Thayendanegea) fought with the British during the Revolutionary War. *(National Archives, Still Picture Records, NWDNS-111-SC-92608)*

THE FIRST AND SECOND BATTLES OF SARATOGA
September 19 and October 7, 1777

Burgoyne easily moved down Lake Champlain and recaptured Fort Ticonderoga on July 6, 1777, but then his problems began. The

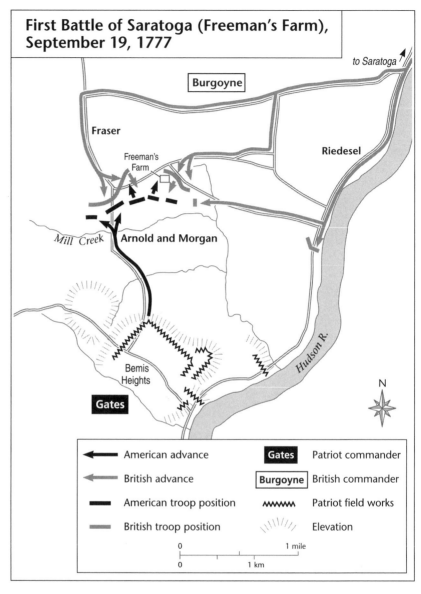

First Battle of Saratoga (Freeman's Farm), September 19, 1777

Burgoyne

to Saratoga

Fraser

Freeman's Farm

Riedesel

Mill Creek

Arnold and Morgan

Bemis Heights

Gates

Hudson R.

N

	American advance	Gates	Patriot commander
	British advance	Burgoyne	British commander
	American troop position	︿︿︿︿	Patriot field works
	British troop position	⑊⑊⑊	Elevation

0   1 mile
0   1 km

The American forces came down from Bemis Heights and defeated the British at Freeman's Farm.

Americans used a number of tactics to delay his progress. Snipers fired at his force, then disappeared into the woods. The Americans also cut down numerous trees that fell into the road between Ticonderoga and Albany that had to be cleared before the army

General Burgoyne surrendered at the Second Battle of Saratoga, as shown in this painting by John Trumbull. *(National Archives/DOD, War & Conflict, #33)*

could move forward. It took Burgoyne's army from June 6 to July 30 to reach the Hudson River from Fort Ticonderoga.

By this time, his supplies were running low, and on August 16, a force was sent out to try and forage for food. They reached Bennington, Vermont, and met a force of New Hampshire militia led by General John Stark, along with Ethan Allen and the Green Mountain Boys. In the Battle of Bennington, on August 16, the British force was nearly wiped out. Rather than returning with much needed supplies, Burgoyne lost irreplaceable soldiers.

On September 13, 1777, Burgoyne crossed to the western side of the Hudson. There he found American general Horatio Gates waiting for him south of Saratoga, New York, where the Americans had fortified the high ground known as Bemis Heights. Gates now

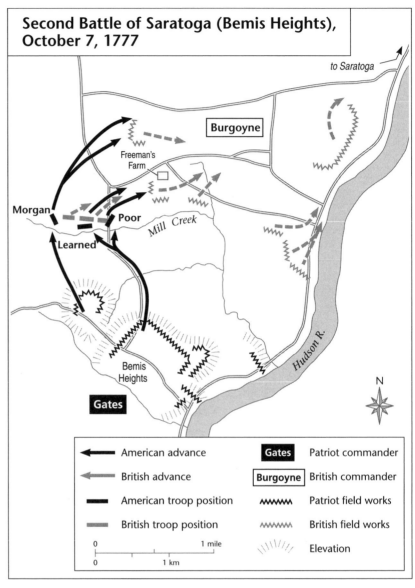

Second Battle of Saratoga (Bemis Heights), October 7, 1777

to Saratoga

Burgoyne

Freeman's Farm

Morgan

Poor

Mill Creek

Learned

Bemis Heights

Hudson R.

Gates

N

	American advance	**Gates**	Patriot commander
	British advance	**Burgoyne**	British commander
	American troop position	∧∧∧∧∧	Patriot field works
	British troop position	∧∧∧∧∧	British field works

0   1 mile
0   1 km

Elevation

Out of desperation, General Burgoyne had the British forces attack the Americans on Bemis Heights. His defeat forced him to surrender, and the war turned in favor of the Americans.

stood in the way of Burgoyne's objective. The British were trapped. They did not have enough supplies to return to Canada and would have to fight the Americans to get to Albany.

Burgoyne split his force into three columns and began to move against Bemis Heights. General Gates kept over half his available force in reserve on the Heights and sent the rest out to engage the British. North of Gates's position, the First Battle of Saratoga was fought at Freeman's Farm on September 19, 1777. On the battleground, the Americans had twice the men of the British. The Americans fought well and took more than 600 British soldiers out of the battle. They only retreated when Burgoyne's third column arrived late in the day.

By October 7, 1777, Burgoyne was in trouble. His force had been reduced to about 5,000 men and the Americans in front of him numbered more than 10,000. Although British general Clinton had begun to move up the Hudson, there was no way he was going to get to Burgoyne in time. Out of desperation, Burgoyne attacked and lost the Second Battle of Saratoga. He was forced to surrender. He and his army were marched to Boston and then sent back to England, promising not to return to the war.

The victory at Saratoga was extremely important. First, it gave the Americans renewed hope that they could defeat the British. And, maybe even more important, it gave the French enough confidence in a potential American victory that they decided to join the war on the American side. Without the aid of the French, the Americans might not have won the War for Independence.

THE REST OF THE REVOLUTION IN NEW YORK

For the rest of the war, New York City and the area around it remained in control of the British. In other parts of the state, there

Taking advantage of the western colonial settlements' weakened defenses as a result of the Revolutionary War, some Loyalists and Mohawk conducted a raid on the Cherry Valley settlement, during which many colonial women and children were killed. Jane Wells, one of the victims, is shown pleading for her life. *(Library of Congress, Prints and Photographs Division [LC-USZ62-111117])*

was almost a condition of civil war as many skirmishes took place between Patriot militia and Loyalists and the Iroquois. As the Revolution was fought in other parts of the colonies, New York attracted numerous Loyalists. New York City had a population of around 5,000 when Washington's army left in 1776. Within a year, there were more than 36,000 people there, mostly Loyalists.

Keeping all these people fed became a difficult task for the British because they were surrounded on all sides by hostile Americans. The only way they had to bring food into the city was by ship. By the end of the war, there was not a tree left standing on Manhattan. They had all been cut down for firewood. During the war years, more than 40,000 people left New York for England or the English colonies in Canada. After the war, many more Loyalists went with them.

10

Postwar Struggles and Building a New Nation

On October 19, 1781, at Yorktown, Virginia, the British commander in North America, General Lord Cornwallis, surrendered. The 13 American colonies had won their independence. While New Yorker John Jay, along with Benjamin Franklin, John Adams, and Henry Laurens, worked in Paris on a peace treaty, British troops remained in New York City. After the victory at Yorktown, George Washington moved what remained of the Continental army to Newburgh, New York. It was a time of great concern in the new United States of America.

THE ARTICLES OF CONFEDERATION

The Second Continental Congress had proposed the Articles of Confederation in 1777. They were finally adopted by the states in 1781. Under the articles, there was a loose confederation of the states and a very weak federal authority. Those who had proposed the articles did not want a strong central government. They wanted the bulk of the power to remain with the states. The experience of the tyrannical abuses of the British government in dealing with the colonies made many leery of giving much, if any, power to a central government.

During the war, the Continental Congress had acted on behalf of the country without real official status. The Articles of Confederation were designed to formalize the union of the 13 separate states. On paper, the articles seemed like a good compromise between those who wanted a stronger federal government and those who did not; however, when implemented, there were numerous problems. The biggest obstacle was that the federal government lacked any way to raise revenue other than by asking the states for money. The federal government also had no way to enforce its laws. In addition, the articles set up a very difficult decision-making process. Each state, no matter its size, was given one

Alexander Hamilton
(1757–1804)

Alexander Hamilton was born in 1757 in the British West Indies and came to New Jersey in 1772 to study at Barber's Academy. He did very well at the academy and entered King's College (now Columbia University) in New York City. On July 6, 1774, he reportedly made his first public speech in which he denounced the British. While still in college, he joined the militia.

When Washington's army came to defend New York in summer 1776, Hamilton was commissioned into the army as an artillery captain. During the war, he rose rapidly and came to the attention of George Washington. Hamilton and Washington became friends, and Hamilton served as Washington's aide-de-camp for part of the war. At the end of the war, Hamilton returned to New York.

Hamilton married Elizabeth Schuyler, a member of a prominent New York family. With his new family connections, Hamilton was able to start the Bank of New York on Wall Street. At this time, he became active in state and national politics. As a New York delegate to the Annapolis Convention in 1786, Hamilton wrote the resolution calling for a constitutional convention to be held in Pennsylvania in the summer of 1787.

At the Constitutional Convention, he was in favor of strengthening the federal government, especially when it came to the federal government taking over the states' debts for the Revolution. When the Constitution was completed, Alexander Hamilton was the only delegate from New York to sign it. The other two delegates, Robert Yates and John Lansing, were reportedly selected for their antifederalist leanings and were instructed to try and keep Hamilton in check.

When it came time for the states to ratify the Constitution, Hamilton was one of the writers, along with fellow New Yorker John Jay and Virginian James Madison, of a series of 85 essays known as the *Federalist Papers*. These essays supported the creation of a stronger federal government and urged ratification of the Constitution. In New York, Hamilton worked long and hard to try and get the Constitution ratified in his home state.

vote. Often delegations could not come to a consensus on an issue and would not be able to cast a vote. This created another problem. The articles required all 13 states to agree before any actions could be taken by the federal government.

Under the Articles of Confederation, at times the 13 states functioned completely independently of each other. Sometimes this put the states in opposition to each other in terms of trade and issues of boundaries. It soon became clear to many that a stronger

Alexander Hamilton's questioning of Aaron Burr's character led to a duel between the two men on July 11, 1804. *(Library of Congress, Prints and Photographs Division [LC-USZ62-75928])*

Alexander Hamilton represented New York at the Annapolis Convention, at which he supported the call for a constitutional convention. *(Library of Congress, Prints and Photographs Division [LC-USZ62-125560])*

federal government was needed. These people became known as federalists, and New Yorker Alexander Hamilton was one of the leaders of the federalist movement. Many people in New York were antifederalist and wanted New York to have the authority to operate as independently as possible. In the years immediately following the war, more and more people came to see the federalists' point of view as the states, federal government, and many individuals experienced financial problems.

Once the Constitution was ratified, and George Washington became the first president, Hamilton served as the country's first secretary of the treasury. In 1795, he returned to New York and stayed active in state politics. When Aaron Burr, who had been an enemy of Hamilton's for a long time, ran for governor in 1804, Hamilton tried to prevent his election. When Hamilton publicly questioned Burr's character, Burr challenged him to a duel. The two met on July 11, 1804, in Weehawken, New Jersey. Hamilton claimed he did not intend to shoot. However, he shot first, wounding Burr. Burr asserted his own gun went off accidentally when he was hit. His shot wounded Hamilton, who died the next day.

LIFE IN POSTWAR NEW YORK

On November 25, 1783, the final British troops in the United States left New York City. Seven thousand Loyalists went with them. All together, it is estimated that 100,000 Loyalists left the United States during or just after the American Revolution. With the British finally gone from New York, the state began to function under its 1777 constitution. During the war, George Clinton had been elected the first governor and had shown himself to be an able leader. After the war, he continued to be elected governor. He served a total of seven three-year terms.

New York City celebrated the evacuation of the British and Loyalist troops on November 25, 1783. George Washington and others paraded down the city streets. *(National Archives/DOD, War & Conflict, #53)*

During the war, Clinton had prosecuted Loyalists and used their confiscated property to supply much needed funds for New York's war effort. In the postwar era, New York continued to go after Loyalists. The state legislature passed a number of laws intended to confiscate the property of Loyalists, even though the Treaty of Paris required that they be left alone.

There was also a very strong antifederalist movement in New York. Twice, New York blocked the attempts of the federal government under the Articles of Confederation to raise money for its support. Financially, New York was better off than its neighbors. It had the best port in North America and after the war fast became the country's busiest harbor.

New York also wanted to maintain control of its own destiny when it came to deal-

George Clinton was elected the first governor of New York during the Revolutionary War. *(Library of Congress, Prints and Photographs Division [LC-USZ62-74112])*

George Clinton
(1739–1812)

George Clinton was from Ulster County, which is about halfway between New York City and Albany on the west bank of the Hudson River. In his political career, he served seven terms as governor of the state of New York and two terms as vice president of the United States. Before being elected governor, he served in the colonial assembly and was a delegate to the Second Continental Congress. He took part in the framing of the Declaration of Independence, but he did not sign it. He had gone back to New York before the signing to assist in the defense of the city. As governor, his policies put New York back on track after the Revolution much faster than many of the other states.

He was a staunch Patriot who had gained military experience in the French and Indian Wars. He was appointed brigadier general in the New York militia. At the time of the Battles of Saratoga, Clinton was able to delay the British forces that were headed north up the Hudson River to relieve General Burgoyne. Due to Clinton's delaying tactics, Burgoyne was forced to surrender to the Americans at Saratoga, and the war turned in favor of the American cause.

When it came time to ratify the Constitution, Governor Clinton strongly supported the antifederalist side. He led the movement in New York to prevent the ratification of the Constitution. If the Constitution had not already been ratified by the required nine states, Clinton and his followers might well have defeated it in New York.

ing with the Native Americans within its borders. During the Revolution four of the Iroquois tribes, the Mohawk, Onondaga, Cayuga, and Seneca sided with the British. After the war many in New York wanted to drive the Iroquois out of the state. Eventually, many of the Iroquois relocated to Canada or moved farther west. Many others were killed during the fighting. New York did not want the federal government interfering with its expansion into what is now the western part of the state.

ANNAPOLIS CONVENTION

By 1786, there were numerous conflicts between the states, especially over commerce. Under the Articles of Confederation, the states were responsible for their own trade regulations. Disputes between Maryland and Virginia over navigation along Chesapeake

Bay and the Potomac River led to the idea that the states should try to amend the articles to give the federal government some ability to regulate trade. Virginia invited all the states to send delegates to Annapolis in September 1786 to discuss the problems.

The states of Virginia, Delaware, Pennsylvania, New Jersey, and New York were the only ones to send delegates. At the convention,

Slavery in New York State

During the Revolution, many slaves in New York earned their freedom by fighting for one side or the other. When the British finally left in 1783, a large number of freed African Americans went with them. These former slaves found freedom in Canada, Britain, the British West Indies, and Sierra Leone. There were also a large number of free African Americans who continued to live in the state. However, there were still 19,000 African Americans who were held as slaves in New York in 1783. To many New Yorkers, the continuation of slavery seemed to be against the principles they had just fought for during the Revolution.

However, the slave owners in New York were not willing to give up their slaves. A bill to end slavery was introduced into the legislature in the mid-1780s, and after many long and heated debates, it passed. However, the law was so flawed that the Council of Revision vetoed it. The bill had allowed for the gradual end of slavery, but the freed slaves would not be granted the same rights as the rest of the people in the state.

The antislavery movement stayed active in the state, and a law ending slavery finally passed in 1799. However, it was not until 1827 that the last slaves in New York State were freed.

British and Loyalist troops evacuated New York City on November 25, 1783. Many freed African Americans were with them. *(Library of Congress, Prints and Photographs Division [LC-USZC4-1306])*

the delegates realized there were two problems. First, they did not have enough states present to accomplish any meaningful changes. More important, they decided that the entire Articles of Confederation needed to be reconsidered and amended to strengthen federal authority.

Alexander Hamilton wrote the convention's report that called for a convention of all the states to be held in Philadelphia in May 1787. The next year, all the states except Rhode Island sent delegates to Philadelphia. The purpose of the convention was to review and amend the Articles of Confederation.

THE CONSTITUTIONAL CONVENTION

When the convention began in Philadelphia in May 1787, it was quickly decided that the articles were too flawed to amend and that the states needed a new federal constitution. Alexander Hamilton was one of the representatives from New York, and he was an active participant in the process. During the writing of the Constitution, numerous debates came up. The most critical of them was the structure of the federal legislature. The large states wanted representation in the legislature to be based solely on population, which would give them the advantage. This idea was known as the Virginia Plan.

The smaller states rallied behind a plan put forward by the delegates from New Jersey that called for each state to be represented equally. To break the impasse between the larger and smaller states, a compromise was suggested by the Connecticut delegation. This became known as the Great Compromise and called for two legislative bodies: a senate in which each state would have two senators, and a House of Representatives that would be based upon population. It is this compromise that ended up in the U.S. Constitution, and it is the way the federal legislature is still organized.

The convention decided that the new Constitution would go into effect as soon as nine states had ratified it. The delegates from Delaware rushed home and became the first state to ratify the Constitution. New York would be the 11th.

RATIFYING THE CONSTITUTION

New York did not rush forward with the process of ratifying the new U.S. Constitution. Some have suggested that Governor Clinton and his antifederalist allies in the state legislature hoped the Constitution would fail in enough other states that New York would not even have to consider it. However, as state after state ratified the Constitution, it became obvious that New York would have to consider it.

The governor called for a state ratifying convention in June 1788. When the convention began to consider the Constitution on June 17, 1788, it looked like there were only 19 federalists out of the 65 delegates. As they began the lengthy process of examining one article at a time, eight states had ratified the Constitution. On June 21, 1788, New Hampshire became the ninth state to ratify, and the Constitution was to become the law of the land.

When news of this reached New York, many members of the convention had to rethink their position. The Constitution had passed, and the question now was whether New York wanted to remain a part of the United States or not. When they finally called for a vote, the convention split with 30 votes for the Constitution and 27 opposed. New York became the 11th state to ratify the Constitution. On April 30, 1789, George Washington became the first president of the United States, and New York City was the nation's first capital. Although New York City did not remain the nation's capital, it became the largest city in North America and the financial hub of the world. New York continues to be an important state in the life of the nation.

New York Time Line

11,000 B.C.

★ Native Americans begin to arrive in present-day New York.

1300 A.D.

★ There are two main Native American groups in New York—the Algonquian and Iroquois.

1524

★ Giovanni da Verrazano sails his ship *Dauphine* into New York Harbor.

1609

★ Samuel de Champlain explores upstate New York and names Lake Champlain for himself.

1609

★ Looking for a trade route to the Far East, Henry Hudson sails the *Half Moon* from Amsterdam to Newfoundland, down along the Atlantic coast to New York, anchoring at the lower end of Manhattan. He also explores Long Island and sails up Hudson River to Haverstraw Bay.

1613

★ Adriaen Block sails in his ship *The Tiger* to New York and trades with American Indians for furs. His ship catches fire, stranding him and his crew who winter on Manhattan. They are helped by the Native Americans who teach them to build wigwamlike shelters. They also explore Connecticut and Rhode Island, leading the Netherlands to claim this large area.

1614

★ The Dutch build trading posts, including Fort Nassau, later called Fort Orange and then Albany.

1621

★ The Dutch West India Company is formed by Dutch merchants, who are given the right to settle and trade with the Native Americans in New Netherland.

1624

★ The Dutch West India Company sends a ship, the *New Netherland*, to New Netherland. Some stay on Manhattan Island, some head north and start Fort Orange, now Albany, the first permanent non-Indian settlement in New York State. Others go to Connecticut, New Jersey, and Delaware.

1625

★ Sarah de Rapaelje is the first child of European parents born in New Netherland.

★ Another ship brings 100 settlers to New Amsterdam along with livestock (including cattle, horses). Fort Amsterdam is built.

1626

★ **May:** Another group of settlers arrives in New Amsterdam, including Peter Minuit, the colony's governor.

1629

★ The Dutch West India Company's Charter of Freedom and Exemptions (Charter of Liberties) establishes the patroon system in New Netherland. They promise to build a fort and to supply slaves. Anyone who pays for 50 people to come to New Netherland would be a "patroon," or landowner.

1638

★ William Kieft is made governor of the colony by the Dutch West India Company. His actions hurt New Netherland's relations with the area's Native Americans.

1640

★ Kieft's War, or the Pig War, takes place. Governor Kieft accuses the Raritan Indians of stealing pigs on Staten Island. He sends 100 men who kill several Raritan, who in turn burn a farm and kill four Dutch men.

1646

★ The first slaves arrive in New Amsterdam.

1647

★ **May 11:** Peter Stuyvesant replaces Kieft as governor. He forms a Board of Nine to help govern. He also tries to turn New Amsterdam around by instituting a fire code and the colony's first police force.

1654

★ The first Jews arrive in New Amsterdam. Stuyvesant denies them the right to worship in 1655.

1657

★ Quakers arrive in New Amsterdam. Some are jailed by Stuyvesant. Stuyvesant is ordered to stop persecuting both the Jews and the Quakers by the Dutch West India Company.

1664

★ James, duke of York, brother of English king Charles II and head of the navy, sends ships under Colonel Richard Nicolls to New Netherland, New Amsterdam.

★ **September 6:** Governor Peter Stuyvesant, outnumbered, surrenders without a fight and Richard Nicolls becomes governor.

1665

★ **February:** The area is officially renamed New York in James's honor.

1674

★ Sir Edmund Andros becomes governor of New York, appointed by James, duke of York.

1685

★ James, duke of York becomes King James II.

1686

★ James II establishes the Dominion of New England, covering all lands from Maine to New Jersey, with Andros as governor. Andros raises taxes and jails protestors. James II bans printing presses and the first House of Representatives.

1687

★ France declares war on England.

1689

★ Captain Jacob Leisler of New Amsterdam takes command of the militia and seizes control of the colony.

1689–97

★ King William's War is fought.

1690

★ **February 8:** Schenectady is attacked by the French and their Native American allies. More than 60 people are killed, and the town is burned.

1691

★ King William III, who comes to power in 1688, sends Henry Sloughter to be governor. On his arrival in March, he arrests

Leisler, his son-in-law, and others for treason. Leisler and his son-in-law are executed on May 16.

★ **May 6:** The New York provincial legislature passes the first six laws, including those to quiet disorders, establish the royal government as the final authority, establish courts, and regulate the militia.

1695

★ The English ask William Kidd, a New York shipowner, to help fight against piracy, which is a real problem for the British, but he is arrested for piracy himself.

1702–13

★ Queen Anne's War is fought.

1725

★ William Bradford begins the *New York Gazette*, the colony's first newspaper, which is pro-British.

1733

★ Bradford's assistant, John Peter Zenger, starts the *New York Weekly Journal*, which is critical of Governor William Cosby.

1734

★ **November:** Zenger is arrested for treason by Governor Cosby.

1735

★ **August 4:** Zenger's trial starts. He is acquitted.

1744–48

★ King George's War is fought.

1754

★ The Albany Congress is held, with representatives from Connecticut, Maryland, Massachusetts, New Hampshire, New York, Pennsylvania, and Rhode Island. The original purpose of the meeting is to discuss fighting the French, but they also discuss their problems with England.

1755

★ **September:** The Battle of Lake George is fought. Major General William Johnson of New York enlists the help of 300 Mohawk and Oneida, who fight with 3,000 militia and defeat the French.

1764

★ The British Parliament passes the Sugar Act, taxing non-British molasses.

1765

★ The Stamp Act is passed by Parliament, requiring stamps on all newspapers and legal documents.
★ **October:** The Stamp Act Congress is held in New York City, with nine colonies represented.
★ The New York Sons of Liberty is formed, led by Alexander McDougall, Isaac Sears, and John Lamb.

1766

★ **March:** The Stamp Act is repealed by Parliament.

1770

★ **January:** The Battle of Golden Hill is fought. The Sons of Liberty fight 60 British soldiers at Golden Hill (now John Street). Several Americans are stabbed by the British with their bayonets.

1774

★ **April 22:** New York holds its own "tea party," and 18 boxes of British tea are dumped into New York harbor.

1775

★ After the Battles of Lexington and Concord on April 19, New Yorkers take control of New York City, and the British leave.
★ **April:** The first provincial congress elections take place.
★ **May 10:** Ethan Allen, Benedict Arnold, and around 80 "Green Mountain Boys" capture Fort Ticonderoga in a bloodless attack "In the name of the great Jehovah and the Continental Congress!"

- ★ **May 12:** Seth Warner, Ethan Allen's cousin, captures the Crown Point, New York, fort with New England troops.
- ★ George Washington becomes commander of the American Continental army.
- ★ **May 23:** The provincial congress meets in New York City.

1776

- ★ **April 13:** General George Washington arrives in New York City, knowing the British will return under General Howe.
- ★ **July 4:** The Continental Congress adopts the Declaration of Independence in Philadelphia. The signers from New York are William Floyd, Francis Lewis, Philip Livingston, and Lewis Morris.
- ★ **July 9:** New York votes to endorse the Declaration of Independence; George Washington orders that the Declaration be read to the troops. A statue of King George III in Bowling Green is toppled, then melted to make bullets.
- ★ **August 27:** The Battle of Long Island is fought. Washington's army of 10,000 troops is defeated by General Howe's force of 20,000 troops, and 1,500 Americans are killed or wounded. The Americans escape to Manhattan by boat.
- ★ **September 12:** Washington begins the evacuation of New York City, moving north.
- ★ **September 15:** The British gain control of most of Manhattan.
- ★ **September 16:** Washington defeats Howe at Harlem Heights, slowing the British down.
- ★ **September 20:** Fire destroys roughly one-quarter of Manhattan.
- ★ Nathan Hale from Connecticut is arrested by the British as a spy.
- ★ **September 22:** Hale reportedly says, "I regret I have but one life to lose for my country" shortly before he is hanged by the British.

1776–83

- ★ The British hold New York City for the next seven years. It becomes a haven for Loyalists.
- ★ Ninety-two of the 308 Revolutionary War battles take place in New York State, more than any other colony except South Carolina.

1777

★ **July 5:** The American General St. Clair abandons Fort Ticonderoga, which falls to the British, who also gain Skenesborough and Fort Anne.

★ **July 27:** Settler Jane McCrea is murdered by Burgoyne's Native American allies. Her death galvanizes American support.

★ **August 6:** Near Oriskany, the American general Nicholas Herkimer's forces fight the British under St. Leger. The British retreat (Herkimer dies later of his wounds).

★ **September 19:** The First Battle of Saratoga (Freeman's Farm) is fought. The British general Burgoyne's forces are defeated by the American Patriots under General Daniel Morgan and Colonel Henry Dearborn.

★ **October 7:** The Second Battle of Saratoga (Bemis Heights) is fought. General Burgoyne's forces attack again, losing 600 to the 150 Americans under Gates and Arnold. This battle is considered a turning point in the war.

★ **October 17:** The Convention of Saratoga is held. Burgoyne surrenders his 5,000 troops to General Horatio Gates.

1779

★ Iroquois leader Joseph Brant, a British supporter, leads a series of attacks against the Americans in central and western New York.

★ **August 29:** Americans under Generals John Sullivan and James Clinton defeat the Iroquois and the British at Newtown, near Elmira. There were 500 Iroquois in the battle primarily from the Seneca and Cayuga tribes. However, the Mohawk leader Joseph Brant and loyalists from the other Iroquois tribes also fought at Newtown. Clinton then lead raids against the Seneca and the Cayuga.

1781

★ **October 19:** The British general Charles Cornwallis surrenders to General Washington at Yorktown, Virginia, the final battle of the war.

1783

★ **January:** The Articles of Peace are signed.

★ **September 3:** The British and the Americans sign a peace treaty in Paris.

★ **November 25:** Evacuation Day—George Washington and his troops replace the British in New York City.

1785

★ **January 11:** New York City begins to serve as the nation's capital.

1787

★ The Constitutional Convention meets in Philadelphia. New York's representatives are Alexander Hamilton, Robert Yates, and John Lansing.

1788

★ **June 17:** A convention is held in Poughkeepsie to consider ratifying the U.S. Constitution (there is considerable debate in New York).

★ **July 26:** At the New York convention, delegates vote 30-27 to ratify the Constitution after hearing that Virginia had ratified it.

1790

★ **August 12:** New York City is replaced as the nation's capital.

New York Historical Sites

ALBANY

Schuyler Mansion State Historic Site   This house, completed in 1763, was built by Philip Schuyler.

   Address: 32 Catherine Street, Albany, New York 12202
   Phone: 518-434-0834
   Web Site: www.nysparks.com/parks

BEAR MOUNTAIN

Fort Montgomery State Historic Site   Fort Montgomery was captured by the British in October, 1777, after a battle where roughly half the Americans were killed.

   Address: Bear Mountain State Park, Bear Mountain, New York
      10911
   Phone: 845-786-2701 x 226
   Web Site: www.nysparks.com/parks

CROWN POINT

Crown Point Historic Site   Crown Point was the scene of numerous battles during the French and Indian wars, and the fort was later captured by the American militia. The ruins are open to the public.

Address: 739 Bridge Road, Crown Point, New York 12928
Phone: 518-597-4666
Web Site: www.nysparks.com/parks

CUTCHOGUE

Old House, Cutchogue Village Green   The Old House, built in 1649, is the oldest English Tudor–style house in New York.

Address: Route 25, Cutchogue, New York 11935
Phone: 631-734-6977

EAST ROCKAWAY

East Rockaway Grist Mill Museum   This 300-year-old gristmill has exhibits on Native Americans, farm life, and schooling.

Address: Wood & Atlantic Avenue, Memorial Park, East
    Rockaway, New York 11518
Phone: 516-887-6300
Web Site: www.geocities.com/wormywart/
    gristmillphoto.html

FONDA

Kateri Shrine   This is the site of the excavated Mohawk village Caughnawaga and the shrine commemorates Kateri Tekakaitua (1656–1680). She was a Mohawk who converted to Catholicism and is still revered by many.

Address: Route 5, Fonda, New York 12068
Phone: 518-853-3646
Web Site: www.katerishrine.com

GERMANTOWN

Clermont State Historic Site   Clermont was the home of the Livingston family for eight generations. It was built by

Robert R. Livingston, who was the first U.S. minister of foreign affairs.

Address: One Clermont Avenue, Germantown, New York 12526
Phone: 518-537-4240
Web Site: www.nysparks.com/parks

GRAFTON

Bennington Battlefield State Historic Site   The Americans under Brigadier General John Stark and Colonel Seth Warner defeated the British under General John Burgoyne in Bennington, just over the border from New York in Vermont.

Address: Grafton Lakes State Park, P.O. 163, Grafton, New York 12082
Phone: 518-686-7109
Web Site: www.nysparks.com/parks

HURLEY

Hurley Stone Houses   This village is 330 years old, and it has 25 of the oldest private houses in the country, which are open to the public on the second Saturday in July.

Address: 17 Main Street, Hurley New York 12443
Phone: 845-331-4121
Web Site: www.hurleyheritagesociety.org

JOHNSTOWN

Johnson Hall State Historic Site   Known for his extensive trading with the Native Americans, Sir William Johnson began the design for this house in 1763, which was built shortly after. He lived here with his Mohawk wife, Molly Brant.

Address: Hall Avenue, Johnstown, New York 12095
Phone: 518-762-8712
Web Site: www.nysparks.com/parks

KINGSTON

Senate House State Historic Site   New York's first Senate met at this state house.

> *Address:* 296 Fair Street, Kingston, New York 12401
> *Phone:* 845-338-2786
> *Web Site:* www.nysparks.com/parks

LAKE GEORGE

Fort William Henry Museum   The site of a battle during the French and Indian wars, it is also the location for *The Last of the Mohicans* by James Fenimore Cooper.

> *Address:* Route 9, Lake George, New York 12845
> *Phone:* 518-668-5471
> *Web Site:* www.fortwilliamhenry.com

New York Independence Trail   This is a self-guided tour of some of the battles of the French and Indian wars and American Revolution.

> *Address:* 66 Sewell Street, Lake George, New York 12645
> *Phone:* 866-OUR-TRAI (866-687-8724)
> *Web Site:* www.independencetrail.org

LITTLE FALLS

Herkimer Home State Historic Site   General Nicholas Herkimer started this house around 1764. He is best known for leading the American troops who were ambushed at Oriskany.

> *Address:* 200 State Road 169, Little Falls, New York 13365
> *Phone:* 315-823-0398
> *Web Site:* www.nysparks.com/parks

LIVERPOOL

Sainte Marie Among the Iroquois Living History Museum
This museum depicts life in the 17th century among the French Jesuits and Iroquois.

Address: 6680 Onondaga Lake Parkway, Route 370, Liverpool, New York 13088
Phone: 315-453-6767

New Rochelle

Thomas Paine Cottage   Thomas Paine built this house for himself.

Address: 20 Sicard Avenue, New Rochelle, New York 10801
Phone: 914-633-1776

New York City

African Burial Ground   The African Burial Ground is an African-American cemetery dating from before the Revolution. There is public art next to it that commemorates it.

Address: 290 Broadway at Duane Street, New York, New York 10048
Phone: 212-337-2001

Federal Hall National Monument   Federal Hall was the first capital of the United States and is where George Washington was inaugurated president.

Address: 26 Wall Street, New York, New York 10005
Phone: 212-825-6888
Web Site: www.nps.gov/feha

Fraunces Tavern Museum   This is a museum with rooms depicting the 18th and 19th centuries in New York City.

Address: 54 Pearl Street, 2nd Floor, New York, New York 10004
Phone: 212-425-1778
Web Site: www.fraucestavernmuseum.org

Lefferts Homestead   The Lefferts Homestead is an early-American farm designed to show children about life then. It has period rooms, exhibits, and games.

Address: Flatbush Avenue at Empire Boulevard, Brooklyn, New York 11215

Phone: 718-965-8951

Morris-Jumel Mansion Museum   The Morris-Jumel Mansion is the oldest house in Manhattan, built in 1765, and is now a museum of New York City history.

Address: 65 Jumel Terrace, New York, New York 10032

Phone: 212-923-8008

Web Site: www.morrisjumel.org

Old Stone House Historic Interpretative Center   This house was reconstructed with the original stones and depicts life in 1776 during the Battle of Brooklyn.

Address: 336 Third Street, Brooklyn, New York 11215

Phone: 718-768-3195

Wyckoff Farmhouse Museum   The Wyckoff Farmhouse Museum offers a year-round program of on-site school and summer camp visits at this historic house that dates to the early period of Dutch settlement in New York.

Address: 5186 Clarendon Road, Brooklyn, New York 11203

Phone: 718-629-5400

Web Site: www.wyckoffassociation.org/museum/
educational.html

NEWBURGH

Washington's Headquarters State Historic Park   George Washington was headquartered in Newburgh from 1782–83.

Address: Liberty & Washington Streets, Newburgh, New York 12551

Phone: 845-562-1195

Web Site: www.nysparks.com/parks

Old Bethpage

Old Bethpage Village Restoration   The Old Bethpage Village Restoration is a living-history museum showing how life was lived on farms and towns. It has 55 buildings open to the public.

Address: Round Swamp Road, Old Bethpage, New York 11804
Phone: 516-572-8400
Web Site: www.oldbethpage.org

Oriskany

Oriskany Battlefield State Historic Site   Thought to be one of the bloodiest battles during the American Revolution, there are signs that interpret the battle site, as well as a historic encampment.

Address: 7801 State Road 69, Oriskany, New York 13424
Phone: 315-768-7224
Web Site: www.nysparks.com/parks

Oyster Bay

Earle-Wightman House Museum   The Earle-Wightman House was built in 1720 and has a 1740 kitchen.

Address: 20 Summit Street, Oyster Bay, New York 11771
Phone: 516-922-5032
Web Site: members.aol.com/obhistory

Raynham Hall Museum   The Raynham Hall Museum was the Townsend family home in the 18th century. It was used as the British headquarters during the American Revolution.

Address: 20 West Main Street, Oyster Bay, New York 11771
Phone: 516-922-6808

PORT JERVIS

Fort Decker   Fort Decker is a Revolutionary War site that has an 18th-century historic house.

>   *Address:* 127 Main Street, Port Jervis, New York 12771
>   *Phone:* 845-856-2375
>   *Web Site:* www.minisink.org

POUGHKEEPSIE

Clinton House State Historic Site   Thought to be where discussions took place on the ratification of the U.S Constitution in 1789, this stone house was built in 1765.

>   *Address:* P.O. Box 88, 549 Main Street, Poughkeepsie, New
>   York 12602
>   *Phone:* 845-471-1630
>   *Web Site:* www.nysparks.com/parks

RENSSELAER

Crailo State Historic Site   Crailo is thought to have been built in the early 18th century by Hendrick Van Rensselaer, grandson of the original patroon. It is now a museum on the life of the Dutch in the upper Hudson Valley during the days of patroonship.

>   *Address:* 9½ Riverside Avenue, Rensselaer, New York 12144
>   *Phone:* 518-463-8738
>   *Web Site:* www.nysparks.com/parks

ROME

Fort Stanwix National Monument   The Americans were able to withstand the British during a 21-day siege at Fort Stanwix in August 1777. The fort has been reconstructed and is a national monument.

>   *Address:* 112 E. Park Street, Rome, New York 13440
>   *Phone:* 315-336-2090
>   *Web Site:* www.nps.gov/fost

Rotterdam Junction

Mabee Farm   Mabee Farm has the oldest farmhouse in the Mohawk Valley, built in 1680, as well as a 1720 inn, 1760 barn, and farming exhibits.

> *Address:* 1080 Main Street, Route 5S, Rotterdam Junction, New York 12150
> *Phone:* 518-887-5073
> *Web Site:* www.schist.org/mabee.htm

Saint Johnsville

Fort Klock Historic Restoration   Fort Klock is a reconstructed Native American trading post of 1750.

> *Address:* Route 5, Saint Johnsville, New York 13452
> *Phone:* 518-568-7779
> *Web Site:* www.fortklock.com

Schoharie

Old Stone Fort Museum   Housed in a 1772 church, the museum has displays depicting 300 years of life in rural New York. There are also seven historic buildings.

> *Address:* 145 Fort Road, Schoharie, New York 12157
> *Phone:* 518-295-7192
> *Web Site:* www.theoldstonefort.org

Setauket

Thompson House   The Thompson House was built in the 17th century and shows how families lived on Long Island at the time.

> *Address:* North Country Road, Setauket, New York 11733
> *Phone:* 631-692-4664
> *Web Site:* www.splia.org

Southold

Southold Historical Museums   The Southold Historical Museums are a collection of colonial and Victorian houses open to the public.

> *Address:* 54325 Main Road, Prince Building, Southold,
>   New York 11971
> *Phone:* 631-765-5500

Staten Island

Conference House   Benjamin Franklin, John Adams, among others, attended the 1776 Peace Conference at the Conference House, built around 1670.

> *Address:* 7455 Hylan Boulevard, Staten Island, New York
>   10307
> *Phone:* 718-984-2086
> *Web Site:* www.theconferencehouse.org

Stillwater

Saratoga National Historical Park (Saratoga Battlefield)   The Battle of Saratoga was fought at this site.

> *Address:* 648 Route 32, Stillwater, New York 12170
> *Phone:* 518-664-9821 ext. 224
> *Web Site:* www.nps.gov/sara

Stony Point

Stony Point Battlefield State Historic Site   This is the site of a Revolutionary War battlefield.

> *Address:* Park Road, Stony Point, New York 10980
> *Phone:* 845-786-2521

SOUTHAMPTON

Thomas Halsey House   The Thomas Halsey House was built in 1648 and is filled with 17th- and 18th-century furniture, ceramics, and textiles.

> *Address:* 249 South Main Street, Southampton, New York 11969
> *Phone:* 631-283-2494

TARRYTOWN

Philipsburg Manor   Philipsburg Manor is a replica of an 18th-century working farm with a gristmill and farm animals.

> *Address:* Route 9, Tarrytown, New York 10591
> *Phone:* 914-631-3992

TICONDEROGA

Fort Ticonderoga   This fort from the American Revolution is open to the public and includes a museum and gardens.

> *Address:* 30 Fort Ti Road, Ticonderoga, New York 12883
> *Phone:* 518-585-2821
> *Web Site:* www.fort-ticonderoga.org

VAILS GATE

Edmonston House   This house, built of stone in 1755, is fully restored and has a blacksmith shop as well as slave quarters. It is also the headquarters of the National Temple Hill Association.

> *Address:* 1042 Route 94, Vails Gate, New York 12584
> *Phone:* 845-561-0855
> *Web Site:* www.nationaltemplehill.org

Knox's Headquarters State Historic Site   This 1754 house was used as Knox and Gate's headquarters during the Revolutionary War.

> *Address:* Route 94, Forge Hill Road, Vails Gate, New York 12584
> *Phone:* 845-561-5498
> *Web Site:* www.nysparks.com/parks

New Windsor Cantonment State Historic Site   Washington had his 1782 winter headquarters in New Windsor, where close to 600 log huts were built into a "cantonment." Staff in period dress demonstrate camp-life activities.

> *Address:* P.O. Box 207, Vails Gate, New York 12584
> *Phone:* 845-561-1765
> *Web Site:* www.nysparks.com/parks

VICTOR

Ganondagan State Historic Site   Ganondagan is the site of a 17th-century Seneca town that had a palisaded granary called Fort Hill. A Seneca longhouse has been re-created, and a series of trails have been laid out with signs with information on Iroquois beliefs and customs.

> *Address:* P.O. 239, 1488 Victor-Bloomfield Road, Victor, New York 14564
> *Phone:* 585-924-5848
> *Web Site:* www.nysparks.com/parks

WHITE PLAINS

Washington's Headquarters Museum/Miller Farmhouse   This house, built by the Miller family in 1738, was Washington's headquarters before the battle at Miller Hill at the end of the Battle of White Plains on November 1, 1776.

> *Address:* 140 Virginia Road, White Plains, New York 10603
> *Phone:* 914-949-1236
> *Web Site:* www.westchestergov.com/parks

YONKERS

Philipse Manor Hall State Historic Site   Frederick Philipse was a well-known Loyalist in New York. His house is now open to the public as a museum.

> *Address:* Warburton Avenue and Dock Street, P.O. Box 496,
>   Yonkers, New York 10702
> *Phone:* 914-965-4027
> *Web Site:* www.nysparks.com/parks

YOUNGSTOWN

Old Fort Niagara State Historic Site   At the mouth of the Niagara River, Fort Niagara was controlled by the French, British, and the United States in turn over a 300-years period.

> *Address:* P.O. 169, Youngstown, New York 14174
> *Phone:* 716-745-7611
> *Web Site:* www.nysparks.com/parks

Further Reading

BOOKS

Doherty, Craig A., and Katherine M. *The Iroquois*. New York: Franklin Watts, 1991.

Fradin, Dennis B. *The New York Colony*. Chicago: Children's Press, 1988.

Kallen, Stuart A. *New York*. San Diego, Calif.: KidHaven, 2002.

Kammen, Michael. *Colonial New York: A History*. New York: Oxford University Press, 1975.

Klein, Milton M., ed. *The Empire State: A History of New York*. Ithaca, N.Y.: Cornell University Press, 2001.

Woog, Adam. *New York*. San Diego, Calif.: Lucent Books, 2002.

WEB SITES

Gotham Center for New York City History. "Gotham History." Available online. URL: www.gothamcenter.org. Updated in 2001.

Hudson River Maritime Museum. "The Hudson River Maritime Museum: Information about the Museum, Events, and Exhibits." Available online. URL: www.ulster.net/~hrmm. Updated in October 2003.

New Netherland Museum. "New Netherland Museum." Available online. URL: www.newnetherland.org. Downloaded on November 10, 2003.

New York History Net. "S.H.I.P." Available online. URL: www.nyhistory.com/SHIP/index.htm. Downloaded on November 10, 2003.

New York State Department of State. "Get the Facts about New York State." Available online. URL: www.dos.state.ny.us./Kidsroom/menupg.html. Downloaded on November 10, 2003.

Index

Page numbers in *italic* indicate photographs. Page numbers in **boldface** indicate box features. Page numbers followed by m indicate maps. Page numbers followed by c indicate time line entries. Page numbers followed by t indicate tables or graphs.